The Authentic Parent:

Developing Your Natural Gifts to Become the Parent You Always Wanted to Be

By
Dr. Jamie D. Kirkpatrick, LMFT
Dominique Ann Silvas, M.A.

Be True To Yourself! J.D.

PUBLISH AMERICA

PublishAmerica
Baltimore

Dominique Silvas

First printing

At the specific preference of the author, PublishAmerica allowed this work to remain exactly as the author intended, verbatim, without editorial input.

ISBN: 1-4241-0441-6
PUBLISHED BY PUBLISHAMERICA, LLLP
www.publishamerica.com
Baltimore

Printed in the United States of America

This book is for all the children who
have touched our hearts, minds, and souls.

In memory of:
Anthony
Noah
Dale

Acknowledgments

In writing this book, we have been transformed by the arduous, but wonderful and invigorating process of becoming authentic. We dedicated ourselves to being real and genuine as we completed this undertaking, although it may have been somewhat painful at times. This journey would have been much more difficult if we had not had the support of some key people in our lives.

Therefore, we would like to thank all those who contributed in various ways to the writing of this book: Scot Silvas, Justin Brady, Sierra Silvas, Maya Silvas, Gearil Hill, Grant Ryan, Michelle Rancour, Diana Silvas, Alexandra Silvas, Lani Long, Deborah Lee, Diana Herrington, Zoila Adams, and all the parents who have survived our classes and workshops, as well as those who have come before us and whose shoulders we stand upon.

The Authentic Parent:
Developing Your Natural Gifts to Become the Parent You Always Wanted to Be

"...the little girl decided that she could not stand to hear the butterfly struggling, so she broke open the cocoon and released the butterfly. The butterfly soared to the ceiling and fell dead to the floor. It is the fluttering of the wings against the cocoon that gives the butterfly the strength it needs to fly."

-Unknown

Introduction

"The road to happiness lies in two simple principles:
find what interests you and that you can do well,
and when you find it, put your whole soul into it—
every bit of energy and ambition and natural ability you have."
-John D. Rockefeller III

As you know, parenting is the most important and most challenging thing you will ever do. You have a precious life in your hands, and with that blessing emerges the most serious responsibility you will ever face. Children are the products of their individual characteristics and what they experience in their formative years. As parents, you have the power to make that experience a healthy one or a damaging one.

Many people are resistant to learning about parenting, due to the meanings they ascribe to this sort of education. We often hear statements such as, "I'm not a bad parent. I don't need to read that." Or, "I don't need anybody telling me how to raise my kids." However, many of the best parents read about parenting because they are growth-oriented and they are concerned with being an *exceptional* parent, rather than settling for merely being *good.*

Honest parents know that they could always be better.

The fact is, children do not come with a "how-to" manual and parents are not born with the automatic "know-how" to be an exceptional parent. Regardless of what developmental point in your child's life you are currently engaged in, you can still work to be the parent you always wanted to be. You cannot change what you did yesterday, or last year, or even five or ten years ago, but you can change what you do from this point forward. You must learn the power of being in the moment and concentrate on your veracity in each of those moments.

Our purpose in sharing this book with you is to help you to be the best parent you can be through self-examination and authenticity. Our mission is to educate parents on the intrinsic emotional needs of their children and provide lifelong tools for raising healthy, thriving youngsters throughout their processes of development. The best way for this to happen is for you as the parent to first understand what your unique natural gifts are and which ones you may need to develop further, as well as how you can assist your children in developing their gifts. Our hope is that, as you discover how to build on these innate human characteristics, you will be cultivating your *authentic self*.

Reflection

"The unexamined life is not worth living."
-Plato

The main concept of *The Authentic Parent* demonstrates that skilled, loving parenting begins with being real, genuine, and true to yourself. It is about understanding your self, your history, and your dreams. If you can learn to take care of yourself and simplify your life, nurturing your child's emotional needs will be more easily accomplished. This ability will allow you to provide your children with the acceptance, control, and security necessary to develop into responsible adults, who are capable of having emotionally healthy relationships.

If these needs are not met, however, the consequences can include acting out, destructive behavior, and mental illness in your children. Therefore, exceptional parenting arises from becoming emotionally healthy parents. The same needs of acceptance, control, and security are essential for adults, too. In order for you to fulfill your children's emotional needs, you must first begin with yourself.

It is our contention that no child can be raised in a vacuum. They need a home that is their own and that they can count on. Whether living with their biological nuclear family, with extended family, or in a foster home, children need parents who are attentive to their needs. They need parents who are capable of making a distinction between themselves and their children, as well as between each child within the family.

Parents must be willing to look inside themselves and not only become aware of, but claim the "baggage" from their past. Until parents discover what their own parents did well and what their parents needed improvement on, they will not have the necessary tools or knowledge to equip themselves to raise their own child to his or her fullest potential.

The goal of parenthood then, is to raise your children from completely dependent infants to independent, resilient, flourishing adults. It is your responsibility to provide an environment wherein healthy development and thriving can occur. It is also your responsibility to fulfill the physical and emotional needs of your children until they are able to do so for themselves.

In order to accept this responsibility, you must first be accountable for yourself, for those things you learned when you were children about how to be a parent and subsequently chose to agree to and carry into adulthood. All parents, even those who seem to take parenthood in stride, providing an unconditionally loving and supportive environment for their children, make mistakes.

We believe that people love their families and although some may think it idealistic, even those parents who may have fallen prey to substance abuse, mental illness or any other damaging maladies which may hit the family system, or are abusive and/or neglectful, essentially want their children to grow into healthy adults. They want them to be safe, happy, and successful in their own right, with few exceptions. Keep in mind that it is never too late for improvement. Recall the "Golden Rule" which purports that you are to treat others as you would like to be treated. If you commit to consistently applying this principle to you and your children, you will successfully navigate your path on this journey through parenthood and grow to become the parent you have always wanted to be.

We have designed *The Authentic Parent* to concisely satisfy certain objectives as it motivates you to assess your current situation and discover your most positive attributes as a parent. It is written in a simple, readable format with short chapters so as not to bog the reader down in academic details.

As you proceed you will notice "Remember" and "Reflection" significations with tidbits of information for you to take into consideration. You will also find "Questions to Consider" throughout the book that we suggest you take the time to think about and write down your answers to. They are meant to be thought provoking. Think about discussing them with your spouse, a friend, a relative, your therapist, or even your child.

As you advance through the book, you will have the opportunity to assess your gifts as an authentic parent and gain insight from your own childhood, in order to develop your strengths. You will also have a better understanding of how to master the fulfillment of the critical intrinsic needs of children. As you build on the unique characteristics of yourself and each of your children, you will ascertain how to determine interactional styles that work best in your family.

More specifically, you will be able to identify communication deficits and improve communication skills. As you explore discipline problem areas within your family and recognize the motivations underlying your children's misbehavior, you will be able to create a value-based discipline plan. You will see that all of these objectives can come to fruition, once you learn to simplify your life, truly care for yourself in spite of the life-stresses that often overwhelm parents and invariably correlate to the emotional wounds within each member of your family, and dedicate yourself to growth and authenticity.

Chapter 1

The Gifts of Authentic Parenting

"It is never too late to be what you might have been."
-George Eliot

Authenticity is about fully utilizing your innate *gifts*; the ones that were especially made for you. Every human being has special talents, abilities, and characteristics that exist in unique combinations for every individual. There are many types of gifts, but they only become *strengths* when they are put into practice and developed.

We all know when something feels absolutely natural and when we have done something well. This sense of knowing is exactly how it feels to be using your gifts and converting them to strengths. Just like muscles, the more you exercise your gifts, the stronger they become. In parenting, natural talent becomes a skill only when it is practiced and cultivated. Those characteristics which may not come naturally to you can also be developed to play a positive role in your life as an exceptional parent.

In this world, we often miss out on the moments that make up our lives because of hectic schedules and overwhelming responsibilities. Take the time to figure out who you are as a person—who you are, for instance, as a parent, a friend, an adult child, or a spouse—and you will reap the rewards of a more serene, satisfying, and meaningful life.

If you are not being authentic, then you are merely surviving in a tragic mode of defense. This happens when life is chaotic, usually because of overwhelming stress, and you have not taken the time to discern what your own personal values are. Subsequently, the way you interact with your children and how you discipline them, simply does not make sense. Certainly, if you are enveloped by childhood pain, or current pain as an adult, or are in an abusive relationship, then you are functioning in a mode of defensiveness. Authenticity is the opposite of defensiveness. If you remain defensive then you are not using or developing your gifts (see figure 1).

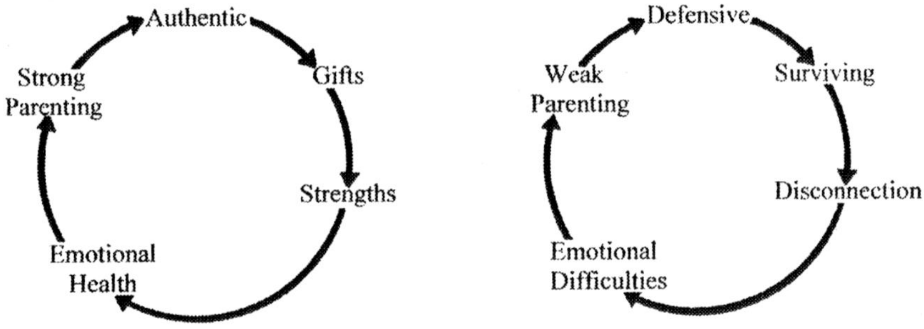

Figure 1. Authenticity vs. Defensiveness. Notice how each way of functioning ultimately cycles around to strong or weak parenting.

Authenticity vs. Defensiveness

The remainder of this chapter focuses on some of the most

common gifts that we have encountered in working with a multitude of parents. As you read through the list, keep an eye on which ones you are strong in and which ones you would like to develop further, perhaps making notes as you go along. In developing your authentic nature as a parent, it is necessary to discover what combination of these and other gifts you already possess and then decide which others you would like to create for yourself.

There are three main categories of gifts which constitute the authentic parent. The first category, **Relationship Gifts**, describes your styles of activity, behavior, and how you interact with others. The second category, **Communication Gifts**, is based on language components and more specifically, how you verbally, physically, and emotionally converse with others. In the third category you will find the **Character Gifts** which are born out of being, state of mind, inner virtues, and personality style. How well you use your gifts with your children dictates how genuine and strong a parent you will be.

Relationship Gifts

♥ **Playfulness**—The gift of playfulness is having a natural aptitude for play. It is the ability to drop everything and truly engage with your children. It is about spontaneity and fun and can come more easily to you when you can tap into your own life as a child.

♥ **Humor**—The gift of humor is an attraction to all things funny. This gift allows parents to make heavy things light, create giggles out of tears, and aids in the art of distraction.

♥ **Tolerance**—The gift of tolerance is the ability to endure all the everyday irritations that go hand-in-hand with parenting. Parents with this gift have a high threshold for noise, mess, and chaos. It affords parents a natural calmness during crises. While it does not involve acceptance of all behaviors, it does involve genuine acceptance of personality and temperament differences between your children.

♥ **Gentleness**—This gift entails a natural softness of voice, touch, gesture, and behavior. Parents with this gift are easy-going and approachable. Children can greatly benefit from a gentle parent's manner and tenderness.

♥ **Generosity**—Parents with this gift are giving of themselves, their time, and their resources. They are also generous in the self-expression of thoughts, feelings, desires, and needs, and easily pass this gift on to their children.

♥ **Fairness**—The gift of fairness allows parents to maintain equality between siblings, while acknowledging individual differences in development, unique capabilities, and gifts. They do not make comparisons between their children or in relation to others, and their expectations are realistic with stable, clarified boundaries. Parents with this gift tend to consistently convey an understanding of right and wrong to their children.

♥ **Healing**—Parents with this gift are natural healers. They can easily dry tears, mend broken hearts, and ease the frustrations of their children. They kiss owies and fix bad-hair days. They are masters of uncovering and repairing old and new wounds.

♥ **Motivation**—The gift of motivation is the innate ability to energize and inspire. Parents with this gift can mobilize children with their creative energy, encouraging them to believe in themselves and accomplish what they need to. They are master planners, coaches, cheerleaders, and task managers.

♥ **Creativity**—The gift of creativity involves a natural artistic take on life. It is the talent to make something out of nothing, or get a toddler to eat their vegetables. Creativity is about freedom in resourcefulness, imagination, and inspiration.

♥ **Flexibility**—The gift of flexibility is about knowing when to bend and when to stand your ground. Flexible parents can make exceptions without "caving-in" on the big issues. They are not rigid and can deal effectively with changes of plans and spontaneity, while maintaining focus.

♥ **Problem Solving**—Parents with this gift have a natural skill to make things work. Their children count on their ability to "fix it" and learn from them how to solve their own problems. They are master teachers who can find a way to proceed no matter what obstacles may lay in their way.

Communication Gifts

♥ **Respect**—Even when they feel angry or frustrated, parents with this gift express themselves with a respectful and caring attitude, rather than being hostile, competitive, or sarcastic. It conveys a genuine appreciation for another simply for being human. Modeling this behavior for your children is the only way they learn to respect themselves and others (especially you).

♥ **Attentiveness**—The gift of attentiveness is the capacity to give one's full consciousness to a child. This gift allows parents to be completely present with their children and convey their children's value and worth by the quality of the parent's vigilance and attention. These parents are self-aware and are in-tune to the child with whom they are trying to communicate.

♥ **Clarity & Directness**—It is important to say what you mean and mean what you say, inquire about another's perceptions, and clarify if need be, so that all messages are accurately perceived and understood. Parents with this gift have a sincere interest in conveying and receiving a message clearly to achieve a genuine connection with their child.

♥ **Teaching**—The gift of teaching is the natural skill to turn any situation into a learning opportunity. Parents with this special talent are a living textbook on life for children with endless curiosity. They learn from their own mistakes, teach their children to do the same, and are open to searching out the knowledge they do not have.

♥ **Listening**—The gift of listening is the natural ease of communication which draws children toward their parents. Parents with this gift have ears which are ready for all the stories, questions, and play-by-plays of their children's lives. They use active listening, paraphrasing their children's words so that understanding is conveyed and so that their perception is clarified, continuously strengthening the bond between child and parent.

♥ **Empathy**—This gift is all about parents who have the ability to walk in their children's shoes. This includes acknowledging what you think your child's probable feelings are, in an effort to open the lines of communication. In an attempt to see the world through his or her eyes, these parents can join in their child's feelings of joy, sadness, pain, fear, and anger. The children of empathetic parents feel understood and validated.

♥ **Understanding**—One step beyond empathy, is the gift of understanding which enables parents to really "get" what is going on with their children. They not only have a good understanding of themselves (both strengths and limitations), but they can also make their children feel understood. These parents know when to give their children space and when their children need to talk. They are approachable even when things go wrong.

♥ **Engagement**—The gift of engagement assures parents that they can "hook" their children into conversation. These parents have a special gift for keeping children talking, tapping into their world, and encouraging discussion. They readily approach their children with empathy and open the channels of communication.

♥ **Compassion**—The gift of compassion signifies a special caring and warmth conveyed through physical and emotional communication from parents to children. Parents with this gift have a natural ability to share such tenderness with their children and let them know how important and valuable they are.

♥ **Genuineness** (Honesty)—The gift of genuineness is about being real. It is the gift of natural sincerity and authenticity. These parents are humble, forgiving, and apologetic when necessary. They are consistent, accountable, and always approachable to their children. Parents with this gift can share their vulnerabilities and emotions with their children without giving up their authority. This parent's approval of the child has no strings attached and the child is assured of the parent's accessibility.

♥ **Inquiry**—Inquiry is about asking gentle, but probing questions with the purpose of learning more about what the other person is thinking and feeling, as well as what their motivations may be. Parents with this gift display a genuine interest in discovering and understanding what is occurring beneath the surface of what they notice in their child's behavior.

♥ **Availability**—Similar to attentiveness, when you practice this gift it lets your child know that you will be there for them when they really need you. You are not invariably too busy for them and you are able to be present in the moment. You and your children are a priority. This adds directly to your child's sense of acceptance and security (discussed in detail in chapter 2).

♥ **Assertiveness**—The gift of assertiveness allows parents to express their feelings openly and directly without being passively or actively aggressive. When interacting with their children, parents with this gift can use assertiveness to be honest *and* direct which is enhancing to them and their children, promoting integrity, respect, and self-competence.

♥ **Calmness**—It can be taxing to communicate effectively, so the calmer you remain, the more likely it will be that all persons involved will feel heard, respected, and find resolution in tense situations. Parents with this gift model self-control and the ability to remain composed in the moment, so that positive emotional interactions can prevail.

Character Gifts

♥ **Patience**—The gift of patience is an inner virtue that allows parents to take a step back when necessary, in order to gain perspective before reacting. Parents with this gift deal with everyday trials with ease and can calmly manage almost anything having to do with their children with grace, tolerance, and dignity.

♥ **Wisdom**—Parents with this gift have insight that translates into honesty and truth. The gift of wisdom allows parents to put a lot of thought into being an exceptional parent. When presented with a challenge, they have a wealth of resources to reach for and will spend ample time searching for possible options to emotional, behavioral, and interactional difficulties.

♥ **Courage**—The gift of courage is about the bravery it takes to be a stand-up parent even in the face of society's opposing ideas. It takes guts to raise a child with wholesome values in today's world of materialism and ethical relativism. Parents with this gift can face their fears and not only teach their children to stand up for what they believe to be true and right, but also become their children's heroes. Courage breeds authenticity.

♥ **Reverence**—The gift of reverence is a natural respect for and a sense of wonder of the world and everything in it. The reverent parent can share the intricacies of a tiny caterpillar with a child, as well as the awesome power of an erupting volcano. They can acknowledge the strength of the human spirit and the blessing of an innocent baby. The point is that this type of parent is modeling an honor for all things and most especially for God, the creator of all.

♥ **Faith**—The gift of faith is about belief and trust. It is a sentiment that signifies to children that everything will be okay. *Someone is looking out for me.* Faithful parents model strength of character and hope.

♥ **Intuition**—The gift of intuition is about rational perception, gut-level apprehension, and understanding. A highly intuitive parent can tune into his or her children's thoughts and feelings before they ever open their mouths to speak. These parents are able to recognize a confused look on their child's face, hear a sad tone in their child's voice, or just have a sense of something not being right with their child. These parents know their children well and have an easier time staying connected. This gift assists parents in empathizing with their child's feelings, reactions, and possible consequences of a given interaction.

♥ **Loyalty**—The gift of loyalty is a natural sense of staying true to those you love and not letting them down. Loyal parents are natural protectors and will always go after the "lost sheep" and protect it from "the wolves." They believe in intimacy, keeping promises, and togetherness. They believe in the concept of *team* in the family and can be counted on to take care of their own.

♥ **Optimism**—The gift of optimism is about thinking in terms of the "glass-half-full." Parents with this gift can turn almost any negative situation around. They practice their gifts of faith and motivation regularly to find the positive in that which is bleak. They help their children to understand, that with the right attitude, there is much to be gained in failure and can therefore, teach them to thrive and persist in all their endeavors.

♥ **Morality**—Parents with a strong, consistent, and innate sense of morality, pass this on to their children. They follow a high moral standard in their own lives, modeling this behavior and sharing life's blessings with their children. They are not hypocrites, rather they practice what they preach, keeping dignity intact for their children through realistic expectations.

♥ **Humility**—The gift of humility is a natural sense that the world does not revolve around you. The humble parent can admit when he or she is wrong, can apologize to children when necessary, and ask for forgiveness. Humility involves having a healthy respect for authority while not becoming self-absorbed.

♥ **Gratitude**—Grateful parents raise grateful children. This gift allows parents to teach their children appreciation for all the bounty in life, to find the beauty in the little things, and not only endure suffering gracefully, but grow from it.

Life can be a difficult journey at times, but the hardships and struggles that we endure teach us lessons. These lessons are hard-won triumphs that guide us when we are faced with new challenges. Each and every difficult situation or encounter holds meaning for us, if in the aftermath we choose to grasp the lesson at hand.

Using your unique gifts, you will become more aware of the learning potential of every experience. When you open yourself to the blessings in your life, your heart will be shaped by the hand of God with every struggle you endure.

Take a moment (or a few) to look back at your life's toughest encounters and notice the lessons hidden in every challenge. Your choice then becomes whether or not you are willing to internalize each lesson, thereby strengthening your gifts, or give up and become a victim of your own life.

Your authenticity is based on your self-honesty. Are you willing to dust off your hidden talents and share your real self with your children? If so, let's get to work and unearth your potential.

Questions to Consider

1. What kind of parent have you always wanted to be?
2. In what parts of your life are you being authentic? In which parts are you not?
3. What are your unique relationship gifts/strengths?
4. What are your unique communication gifts/strengths?
5. What are your unique character gifts/strengths?
6. Which gifts/limitations could you work to strengthen?

Chapter 2

Necessary Nourishment

"There is only one deprivation...and that is not to be able to give one's gifts to those one loves most."
-May Sarton

All people are born with certain needs and innate characteristics as human beings. Some of these are unique to the individual, such as temperament and personality style, while others are universal, such as oxygen to breathe. Each person is born with three fundamental needs which are the foundations of healthy emotional development. These three needs are the need for **acceptance**, the need for **control**, and the need for **security**. They are the building blocks of strong character and resilience and will be explained in more detail in the following pages.

As parents you are your children's teachers, their guides, their playmates, their coaches, their nurturers, and their counselors. As we explained in the first chapter, knowing yourself, as well as your strengths and limitations, will help you create the best physical and emotional environment possible for your children to grow.

The Need for Acceptance

Acceptance is the feeling that one is worthy, cared for, and approved of, simply for being. Children need to be valued and treated as individuals in their own right with their own feelings, opinions, desires, and ideas. Acceptance includes the need to be respected, to be treated with courtesy, consideration, and esteem. When children consistently experience unconditional acceptance they establish a healthy self-ego. They develop a sense of value, usefulness, and confidence.

Thus they are made to feel important and become more aware of their worth, have a positive outlook on life, and feel capable of accomplishing their goals. They are more likely to form positive relationships, are less critical of others, and are more resistant to outside negative influences. Therefore, they are more open to positive adult role models.

Children cannot choose to be in another family and those who do not receive acceptance at home are more likely to find themselves in unsafe situations. That is, they will seek acceptance in unhealthy ways and be less resilient to outside influences (e.g., unhealthy relationships, gangs, drugs, overachieving). Simply put, they are at higher risk for being hurt in a multitude of ways.

Constructive parenting methods of giving children acceptance

- ♥ Respect
- ♥ Mentoring/guidance
- ♥ Courtesy
- ♥ Positive reinforcement
- ♥ Honesty
- ♥ Shared discussions, activities, & chores
- ♥ Encouragement & praise
- ♥ Traditions/rituals
- ♥ Positive attention
- ♥ Giving credit/status
- ♥ Active listening
- ♥ Cooperative decision-making
- ♥ Showing interest
- ♥ Providing forgiveness
- ♥ Validation of thoughts, feelings, & behaviors
- ♥ Genuine sharing of yourself

Destructive parenting methods of withholding acceptance

♥ Suppressing feelings
♥ Criticism/belittling
♥ Being judgmental
♥ Overreacting
♥ Authoritarian parenting
♥ Excessive permissiveness
♥ Secretiveness
♥ Ignoring
♥ Favoritism
♥ Disrespect
♥ Rudeness
♥ Lying
♥ Demeaning behavior
♥ Interrupting/half-listening
♥ Lecturing/advice giving
♥ Over-protectiveness

Common ways children attempt to fulfill their need for acceptance

♥ Clinginess
♥ Lying/exaggerating
♥ Cliques/gang participation
♥ Stealing
♥ Becoming an overachiever
♥ Giving things away
♥ Becoming a "people-pleaser"
♥ Neediness

Adults have the skills to discriminate between situations and people that treat them well or feel accepting, unless acceptance was withheld when they were children. Children however, cannot label rejection—cannot define it. They only know that it feels awful, which leads them to internalize the feelings and believe that they are bad, that they are unlovable and unworthy of acceptance.

Common ways adults attempt to fulfill their need for acceptance

Constructive

♥ Choosing friendships/mates who accept them for who they are
♥ Avoiding situations (e.g., jobs, church, clubs, etc.) in which they might feel unworthy or out of place
♥ Being dependable, loyal, honest, and hard-working on their job

Destructive

♥ Continuing futile attempts to earn love from family or friends who may be emotionally unavailable or incapable of extending acceptance and approval
♥ Knowing what rejection feels like, they avoid risking any trust in others at all cost
♥ Overdoing for others in an effort to "earn" acceptance

Case Example

Jacob, 11 years old, plays the position of Forward for his soccer team, the Lizards. He is having a difficult time meeting his father, Dan's, expectations. No matter how fast he runs or how hard he kicks the ball, he cannot seem to please his father.

"Come on! What are you doing?" Dan yells, as Jacob passes the ball behind one of his teammates. "Run!" Dan screams, "Run!"

Jacob runs to recover the ball from the player on the other team, but cannot reach him in time. He hangs his head in shame, thinking he is not *good enough*. He knows that his father has spent a lot of time working with him in extra practices and he doesn't want to disappoint him. So, he tries harder and harder.

Jacob finally thinks he has a chance to make a goal. He is "wide-open" when his teammate passes him the ball. Jacob attempts to stop it, but the ball swooshes between his legs.

"Jacob!" blasts, Dan. "How did you miss that? It came right to you!"

Not letting on that he is sad and angry with himself, Jacob begins to cry quietly while resuming his play.

"Get it together, boy. You can do better than that. Go after it!"

Jacob continues to run faster and kick harder, but to no avail. The harder he tries to please his father, the slower and less coordinated he becomes. It is just not his day to score.

Although Dan believes that Jacob is more accomplished than his present performance and often tells his son that he is capable of succeeding and doing well, his negative statements during this game counteract these points. Essentially, Dan is telling his son that he rejects him because his performance is not up to par. Dan's love for his son comes across as conditional on Jacob's achievement.

Regardless of Dan's true intentions, the messages that Jacob receives and internalizes from his father during this game is that he is unacceptable—that he can't do anything right. He is not good enough for his father's love. He thinks he is a terrible soccer player and an essentially *bad kid*. These perceptions are likely to generalize to his life if Dan does not start to pay closer attention to the messages he is sending to his son.

By Dan's overtly displaying disappointment when his son could not meet his expectations, Jacob's self-confidence, self-respect, and esteem were affected. He felt more hopeless and thought he was a failure. Eventually, Jacob is likely to lose all optimism and feel helpless, discontinuing reaching for success and ultimately giving up.

Questions to Consider

1. How did your parents respond to your needs for acceptance?
2. Which situations and people in your life now give you a feeling of acceptance?
3. Are there any situations or relationships that you avoid for fear of rejection?
4. How do you respond to your children's needs for acceptance?

The Need for Control

All people have the need to feel in control of their immediate environment, including themselves and their personal space. Control is the ability to restrain, direct, or regulate while having a sense of empowerment over one's own physical being, passions, abilities, and spiritual self. Children, who are given control of their bodies, thoughts, feelings, and personal space, do not seek to control things outside of themselves or to exert power over others. Instead, they build self-confidence, having better relationships with those around them, as well as healthier boundaries.

When children feel out of control of themselves or their immediate environment, they may behave in various unhealthy and undesirable ways in order to regain some of that control. If this need for control is not fulfilled, children feel insecure and powerless, often becoming easily intimidated, withdrawn, frustrated, and/or rebellious. They can appear defiant, stubborn, testy, and miserable. In short, they may have difficulty trusting themselves or others, feeling out of control most of the time.

Constructive parenting methods of giving children control

- ♥ Teaching self-care skills
- ♥ Giving responsibility
- ♥ Showing them how to care for others(e.g., pets, siblings, friends)
- ♥ Letting them make mistakes
- ♥ Providing reasonable choices
- ♥ Giving them their space
- ♥ Recognizing accomplishments
- ♥ Providing routines
- ♥ Setting appropriate limits
- ♥ Clarifying boundaries
- ♥ Apologizing when necessary
- ♥ Extending respect
- ♥ Using discipline designed to teach
- ♥ Using natural & logical consequences
- ♥ Asking for their opinions and thoughts
- ♥ Using cooperative decision-making
- ♥ Responding honestly
- ♥ Being reliable
- ♥ Having a positive and unified relationship
- ♥ Allowing the expression of feelings between parents

Destructive parenting methods of taking away control

♥ Being argumentative/over-controlling
♥ Violence between parents
♥ Inconsistent discipline
♥ Inappropriate/nonexistent limits
♥ Disrespect between parents
♥ Punishment
♥ Alcohol/drug abuse
♥ Invading privacy
♥ Being overprotective
♥ Manipulativeness/dishonesty
♥ Overindulgence
♥ Breaking promises
♥ Removing choices
♥ Abuse/neglect

Common ways children attempt to fulfill their need for control

♥ Engaging in power struggles
♥ Isolation/withdrawal
♥ Ignoring instructions
♥ Not sharing
♥ Fighting with siblings/peers
♥ Being picky
♥ Defiance
♥ Stubbornness
♥ Excessive cleanliness
♥ Being overly achievement-oriented

Most of us have had experiences with one or many parts of our lives becoming out of control. Some examples are: depression, grief/loss, divorce, illness, injury, job loss, the birth of a new child, a spouse having an affair, getting cut off on the freeway, and "9/11." Think about how that feels and what your life would look like without certain controls in place. You would merely be allowing anything and everything to happen to you—you become the ultimate victim. However, most control is illusion. That is, you cannot control what other people feel, do, think, or believe, any more than you can control natural disasters. The *only* thing you can really control as an adult is yourself and your immediate physical and emotional space.

Common ways adults attempt to fulfill their need for control (constructive & destructive)

Constructive

- ♥ Pursuing financial success through employment
- ♥ Planning/Maintaining schedules
- ♥ Organization (e.g., work, home life)
- ♥ Following a healthy diet
- ♥ Exercise
- ♥ Seeking equal-level peer relationships
- ♥ Limit-setting with children or others

Destructive

- ♥ Unnecessary plastic surgery
- ♥ Working diligently to avoid their own parents' influence in adult life
- ♥ Abusing alcohol/drugs
- ♥ Defying authority unnecessarily
- ♥ Dominating mates, children, and others
- ♥ Dieting

Case Example

Consider Peggy, who cannot convince her son, Jason, to long sleeve green button-up shirt. She knows the weather co chilly and wants Jason to be prepared. It's a legitimate concern does not like his green shirt however, and prefers his short-sleeve one. It's his favorite, even though he has grown out of it. The more Pe stands firm in her wise clothing choice, the more Jason fights ba verbally and physically, eventually throwing the green shirt on the floo stomping on it, and running out of the room without a shirt on at all.

In this scenario, Jason probably feels out of control and thus senses the need to struggle with his mother to regain power. Being six years old and facing so many new challenges at this age, he wants to hang onto the things that are stable, predictable, and familiar to him. Peggy is attempting to assert her authority over Jason, stripping him of the power to make his own decision.

So, what is wrong with letting Jason wear the shirt he wants? Is there anything wrong with Peggy wanting him to wear the shirt she chooses? If it gets chilly outside, will Jason become the "ice boy" who freezes solid in some discrete sandbox only to be found 1000 years from now, with archeologists wondering why he is wearing a shirt that is clearly too small for him? Not likely. He may get a little cold and other children might laugh at him for wearing a short-sleeved shirt that is too small for him. However, he will have made his own choice, made his own mistake, and learned from the natural consequences of his decisions. By not struggling with her son, Peggy will have taught him a valuable lesson, while allowing his integrity, self-confidence, and control to remain intact.

Questions to Consider

1. How did your parents respond to your need for control?
2. Which situations and people in your life now give you a feeling of control? What role do you play in this?
3. What situations or relationships in your present life do you feel are out of control? What role do you play in this?
4. How do you respond to your children's need for control?

The Need for Security

rol and the need for security go hand-in-hand this need. Security develops out of providing ency, a safe and caring environment, and s for children. Children who feel secure grow up city to trust themselves and others. They are onfident, and self-reliant.

ertains to both physical security and psychological/ ecurity. As Abraham Maslow (1908-1970) contends, a hysical needs must be met before psychological growth place. We discuss Maslow's *Hierarchy of Motivational* n more detail in Appendix A.

n order for children to feel secure, their basic physical needs ust be met at all times. These needs are food, air, water, shelter, and clothing. The emotional need for security involves such elements as knowing that one has free choice within his or her own personal space, which is not at risk of invasion from others. Children with this need fulfilled know that they are safe at home and can depend on family. They are not walking on eggshells and they feel taken care of.

If parents belittle their child, are inconsistent in expectations, or are emotionally absent due to alcohol or drug abuse, then that child will likely be confused, fearful, withdrawn, and feel helpless. He or she will grow up often feeling intimidated, being indecisive and frustrated in life. The child is liable to have low self-esteem, low self-confidence, and increased shyness. Thus a lack of security can produce a learned helplessness, making it more likely that a child will eventually cease attempts to fulfill this need and will give up, never regaining his or her hope.

Constructive parenting methods of giving children security

- ♥ Providing physical needs
- ♥ Providing routine/structure
- ♥ Giving children their space
- ♥ Emotional and physical availability
- ♥ Being reliable
- ♥ Appropriate limit setting/boundaries
- ♥ Being consistent
- ♥ Providing a strong sense of values
- ♥ Keeping promises
- ♥ Honesty/Genuineness

Destructive parenting methods of taking away security

- ♥ Inconsistent discipline
- ♥ Inappropriate/non-existent limits & boundaries
- ♥ Breaking promises
- ♥ Alcohol/drug abuse
- ♥ Violence between parents
- ♥ Invading child's privacy
- ♥ Physical and emotional neglect
- ♥ Dishonesty
- ♥ Unstable home life
- ♥ Punishment/Abuse
- ♥ Separation/Divorce

Common ways children attempt to fulfill their need for security

- ♥ Isolation/Withdrawal
- ♥ Being achievement-oriented or giving up
- ♥ Engaging in power struggles
- ♥ Rebellion/Defiance
- ♥ Stubbornness
- ♥ Materialism
- ♥ Excessive cleanliness
- ♥ Hoarding and/or not sharing
- ♥ Stealing
- ♥ Clinginess

Common ways adults attempt to fulfill their need for security (constructive & destructive)

Constructive

- ♥ Pursuing financial success through employment
- ♥ Having supportive people in their lives
- ♥ Education
- ♥ Planning, structure, routine
- ♥ Installing a home security system
- ♥ Being consistent in behavior, thoughts, & feelings
- ♥ Excessive cleanliness
- ♥ Relying on friends/family when necessary
- ♥ Decisive decision making

Destructive

- Arguing with spouse over finances
- Being abusive
- Obsessive relationships
- Materialism
- Bullying spouse or children
- Compulsive behaviors
- Addictions
- Perfectionism
- Being a "people pleaser"
- Seeking to have the "last word"

Case Example

Think about Mike and Sharon, parents to 8-year-old Tina and her two younger siblings, Kevin, 6, and Theresa, 4. Mike and Sharon both work, but have been having some financial troubles. They seem to be in conflict with one another almost every night. When they are not openly fighting, they are battling a "cold war," each avoiding and ignoring the other.

Mike and Sharon's arguments include disagreements about the kids, their inability to pay bills, and any little thing that one of them can find wrong with the other. Sharon nags Mike about picking up his shoes in the living room, while Mike complains that dinner is not ready "on time." Mike is angry that Sharon spends money on toys for the children and Sharon moans about Mike so often coming home late from work. On and on it continues, day after day.

Meanwhile, Kevin is wetting his bed a couple of times per week and Theresa is becoming very defiant. Tina cannot sleep and has terrible nightmares. Sometimes her dad pushes her mom and often her mom throws things. Usually her dad leaves the house when it gets really intense and Tina is afraid he will not be there when she wakes up in the morning.

What if they both leave because they can't take care of us anymore? Tina wonders. *What if mom gets hurt?* She cannot stop the thoughts from plaguing her every waking hour. *Who will take care of us?*

When Mike leaves, Sharon tends to turn her negative attention toward the children, nit-picking everything they do. She screams at them or insists that they watch T.V. quietly instead of being in her hair. When Sharon behaves in this manner, Tina does her best to try to take care of her siblings, especially Theresa, just to make sure that they are okay.

In general, Tina and her siblings walk on eggshells regularly, uncertain about what will happen next. Their parents' behaviors are unpredictable and they always feel a bit off-kilter. Tina feels a great deal of unrealistic responsibility for everyone in the family, but does not think that she is adequately fulfilling her roles as daughter and big sister. Therefore, her self-esteem and self-confidence are being thrown into question. Clearly, Tina's inability to sleep due to worry, Kevin's bedwetting, and Theresa's defiance are manifestations and symptoms of a lack of security within this family.

Questions to Consider

1. How did your parents respond to your need for security?
2. Which situations and people in your life now give you a feeling of security? What role do you play in this?
3. What situations or relationships in your present life do you think are not secure? What role do you play in this?
4. How do you respond to your children's need for security?

Emotional needs are the fuels that keep us going. Resiliency, strength of character, and clear boundaries are the precursors of successful, positive relationships and are the direct result of satisfying these emotional needs. Younger children, in particular, are at a very crucial stage and their healthy development depends on whether or not these needs are fulfilled.

Parents also need to consider the fact that their own sense of self and authenticity rest largely on how they fulfill these needs for themselves. Even if parents did not have a near-perfect childhood with parents who consistently understood and fulfilled their needs, it is possible to learn how to satisfy your own needs in adulthood. Start by taking a long hard look at which areas of your life are not working well or are uncomfortable for you, and then take action to fulfill your needs of acceptance, control, and security. Your children will not only learn from your modeling self-care, but you will develop your authenticity and, as a result, be a better parent.

Chapter 3

Ties That Bind

"All happy families resemble one another,
but each unhappy family is unhappy in its own way."
-Leo Tolstoy

This chapter focuses on single parent, blended, and intact family structure, relationship boundaries, and parental roles. Here you will understand the dynamics of well-functioning families and the individual members they are comprised of.

Family Structure

Families can best be understood as systems. They are units made up of unique entities which are interactive and interdependent. In other words, a family is any two people which affect each other by their every action. They are akin to an infant's mobile in which, once you touch one part of the mobile, every other part moves. One part being out of balance creates imbalance throughout the entire system. Nothing can take place with a single member of a family without it affecting every other member, whether noticeably or not. When a system gets out of balance its individual members will do almost anything to regain that balance (e.g., alcohol use, overachievement, infidelity).

Case Example

John had been having trouble lately getting in touch with his wife, Sally, during the day and suspected that she was having an affair. John could not bring himself to ask her directly whether this was the case and merely responded to her by distancing himself or arguing over minor issues. Sally knew there was something wrong, but John refused to speak to her about the problem.

Their children, 15-year-old J.J. and 17-year-old Michelle, both sensed there were problems with their parents, but their parents would not respond to their concerns or answer their questions. In return, the children began avoiding the family. Michelle stayed away by hanging out with friends. J.J. began smoking marijuana and drinking beer with one of his buddies.

John and Sally knew that Michelle was bothered by something and Sally found a joint in J.J.'s shirt pocket. Additionally, Michelle knew that J.J. was drinking and smoking weed, but she protected her brother and did not tell her parents because she did not want to "rock the boat" even more. Michelle was not often around to talk to, but continual arguments ensued between J.J. and his parents. The more John and Sally focused on J.J., the less they had to think about their own problems.

John became increasingly frustrated and began to go out after work for a couple of drinks. In his avoidance of his family's problems, he began to stay out later and later and drink more and more. Communication problems, passive-aggressive behaviors, and defensiveness produced anxiety throughout the family, as both children and parents lived uneasily, avoiding their concerns.

Their family was falling apart, getting chaotic and confusing simply because John and Sally could not communicate their thoughts and feelings. The truth was Sally did not answer her cellular phone because she was taking yoga classes and exercising daily with a friend, in order to get in shape for her and John's twenty-year high school reunion. At these times, she did not take her phone with her.

As you can see, an atmosphere of suspicion makes everyone in the family anxious and throws the system off balance. Each person then attempts to regain balance and get their needs fulfilled by engaging in unhealthy, "acting-out" or "acting-in" behaviors.

Remember

Genuine & open communication
keeps family structure balanced and intact.

Within each family system there are also smaller systems, called subsystems, such as two siblings or a parent and a child, which may form alliances or be in conflict. The Structural Family Therapy Model largely brought about by Salvador Minuchin in the 1970s, was centered on the idea that families tend to be organized hierarchically and are constantly striving to find balance between stability and change within the system. In healthy families, the executive subsystem (husband/wife or single parent) endeavors to remain the strongest authority in the family. In a two-parent household, the husband and wife must display a united front in order for the system to function properly. In a single parent family, the executive subsystem must still be the strongest authority in the household.

The mistake that many parents make, especially in a single parent household, is shifting the power in the home to one side, perhaps becoming enmeshed with one child or scapegoating another child. This behavior changes the balance within the family system and a parent's authority may even become wholly non-existent. In response to this lack of or uneven power, some parents may attempt to inadvertently hand control over to the children or substitute a child for an absent parent. The result is household division and child insecurity.

In all types of families dysfunction appears in the form of sibling rivalry, acting-out/in behavior, parental frustration, parent-child conflict, and marital difficulty. Therefore, when the balance of power is off in the system's hierarchy, emotional and behavioral problems have a trickle-down effect through the family. In figure 2 you can see a depiction derived from Minuchin's hierarchy of the family system.

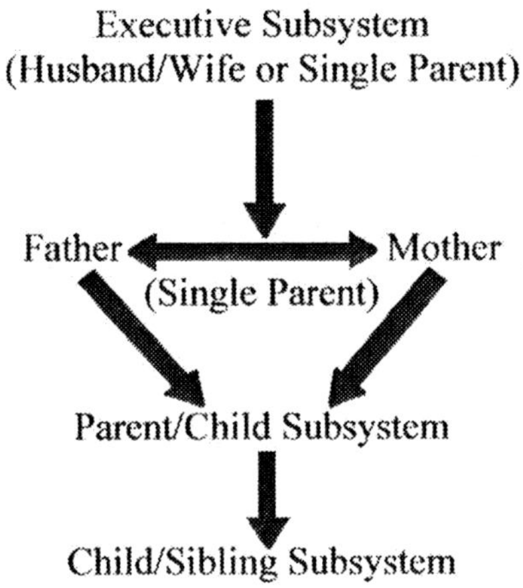

Figure 2. Family System Hierarchy. A healthy balance of power within the family system moves in a downward direction.

Family System Hierarchy

Questions to Consider

1. What alliances do you see have formed within your family system? Where are the divisions?
2. Who in your family holds the authority and if you have a mate, do you function within the executive subsystem from a united front as parents?
3. What does the balance of power look like in your family?
4. What symptoms do you see in your children that may indicate that your family is out of balance (e.g., defiance, depression, sibling rivalry, insecurity)?

Blended Families

Blended families have a multitude of issues confronting them, but it is not impossible to navigate a clear path through the mire of challenges. Regardless of which parent is the step-parent (Mother/ Father) their roles do not differ widely. The blended family still faces certain challenges regardless of the ages of the children involved, although how the parents manage these challenges may depend somewhat on the children's ages at the beginning of the new marriage. Therefore, it is important to become aware of the possible obstacles within the blended family when considering the functional roles of the marital relationship and individual parents:

♥ **Main roles of biological parent:** Emotional and physical safety net; nurturer; disciplinarian.

♥ **Main roles of step-parent:** Respectful adult; friend; tolerant consultant.

Blended families have special issues, but the needs of the children remain the same. Acceptance by the step-parent is essential. Having a sense of security and a sense of control over their lives is paramount to children, but most often these are the first to go during and after a divorce.

Remember that the fear and chaos of divorce do not last forever. Children are more capable of healthy functioning and development coming from a broken home than they are living in one. However, keep your eyes on the goal, which is *not* winning or making the other parent pay. The goal is always to nurture a happy, healthy, well-adjusted child/adolescent/adult. There will be emotional battle scars, but you can help your children cope through the pain, fear, grief, and insecurity and not only survive it yourself, but eventually learn to thrive.

Remember

Step-parents must first be friends to their step-children, not disciplinarians.

The most important factors in successful blended families are flexibility and negotiation. Master these skills with your ex-spouse, the new step-parent, and your child to ensure that everyone involved will eventually adapt and adjust to the new family system.

Blended families are the most challenging of all balancing acts, so authenticity plays a huge role. Not only do blended families have the unique challenges of childhood and adolescence to face with each child, but they have a host of new and complicated issues to deal with regarding the new family structure and new members.

One of the most important strategies is staying true to yourself throughout every new ordeal. Your roles as a parent, spouse, step-parent, and individual take on entirely different dimensions than within an original intact family system. Successful blended families that have struggled through the changes and remained together have spent a lot of time building separate relationships, and working on their own self-awareness. Understanding your own strengths and limitations is key in working out your challenges in a blended family.

While all the gifts will certainly enhance the relationships in any blended family, it is important to isolate and identify those which come most naturally to you and develop them. Honest communication, clear boundaries with your significant other, and a whole lot of patience and compassion for the child or children who have just become a part of your life, are essential to success.

Remember

Do not expect your children
to immediately accept and adapt
to new family members.

Four of the most common difficulties that arise among blended families are *resentment, insecurity, rejection,* and *jealousy*. These challenges interfere with one's authenticity and play havoc with a person's emotions. It is nearly impossible to use your strengths when you get lost in these problematic areas. It is natural when feeling resentful, insecure, rejected, or jealous to bring all of your most formidable defenses to the forefront. However, these defensive responses are exactly what destroys relationships and hurts the people you love the most.

Sarcasm, ignoring, passive aggression, and martyrdom are common defensive traps that step and biological parents fall into when things get tough in blended families. The antidote for the various problems that arise is always to take a step back and check in with yourself. This assures that you will not instantaneously respond with emotional reactivity. You must then come from a place of authenticity and use your gifts instead of your defenses. It is necessary to keep perspective and not get caught up in everyday problems. Your relationships are the most important thing in your life. They are precious and priceless and nothing can replace them.

The ultimate goal is for the blended family to become strong as a new system and for the children and adults in the family to grow in their love and respect for each other as healthy individuals. Losing sight of this goal and getting stuck in a win/lose mentality is setting yourself up for failure, because everyone will lose. The balance of power is a very intense challenge and needs to be thought out and dealt with in a mature and loving way by the parents.

You will find in chapter 9 that one of the most important facets to creating a strong family system is history. Memories are a vital component of family history. Pictures, stories, and traditions help hold families together and create a sense of belonging and acceptance. In essence then, building a history together in a blended family (as in any family) is one of many tasks that need to be accomplished in order to strengthen family ties.

Reflection

Children from divorced families
have the most positive outcomes
when the biological parents have ended the battle
and learned to cooperate.

Flexibility, negotiation, and forgiveness are the three skills essential to ending the battle after a divorce, as well as co-parenting successfully. In order to survive any kind of custody arrangement, being willing to work with the other parent is the key. Things are not always going to go as planned. Traditions and routines will be turned upside-down and inside-out. Rigidity will *not* work! It will serve only to make you miserable and your divorce and custody battle will consume you. It is invariably best for the children and the ex-spouses to work with each other, allow for changes, and remain flexible whenever possible. Negotiation skills become an art form of the highest order. Co-parents who master these skills have children with the most positive outcomes.

In a perfect world, flexibility and negotiation skills would be passed out in family court like party favors. Unfortunately, these priceless qualities are traditionally learned over time through trial and error, if at all. Making the effort to strengthen these skills, however, is well worth the work since it is your children who are the real victims when you are involved in a perpetual battle with the other parent. Regardless of which parent seemingly "wins" the battle, the children inevitably lose.

Remember

The other parent is not perfect and neither are you.
If there were not communication and other problems before,
you would probably still be married.
Do not expect perfection; simple progress is enough.

Achieving forgiveness is the final necessary hurdle in the battle of the divorced and blended family scenario. It is not easy, but it is of absolute necessity. It is important to keep in mind that forgiveness is not about releasing the other party from responsibility for his or her unwarranted, negative behaviors. It is about understanding his or her humanity and releasing yourself from the chains of the grudge. Do not forget that you did once care for this person and your children still do. There can be justice in this life and the next, but it is not up to you to impose that justice on those who hurt you.

The release found in forgiveness has great benefits on you and those closest to you. Holding on to anger and resentment based in pain and sadness serves only to punish yourself. It works its way inside and can destroy your life, your health, your parenting, and ultimately, your children.

Reflection

"Always forgive your enemies.
Nothing annoys them so much."
-Oscar Wilde

Letting go and learning to forgive comes from first grasping the lessons to be learned throughout the process and then moving forward. Even an ugly, abusive relationship that ends in catastrophe and major drama has the ability to teach you something about life and yourself. Our advice: make the effort to forgive, grab the lesson, and move on.

Remember

Forgiveness follows learning and acceptance.

Questions to Consider

1. What issues are you currently dealing with as the biological or step-parent?
2. How are these related to the bigger challenges of insecurity, resentment, rejection, and jealousy?
3. What can you do today to improve your skills of flexibility, negotiation, and forgiveness?
4. If you are in a blended family, what roles do your gifts play in this system? Are you using them to their fullest potential? Or are your defenses getting in the way?
5. If you are divorced and not yet in a blended family situation, how can you use your gifts to prepare yourself for taking this step?

Relationship Boundaries

Boundaries are lines of demarcation that separate individuals from each other and separate the family from the outside environment. They may be rigid (closed), diffuse (open), or well-defined and clear. The purpose of maintaining protective boundaries is to protect the fundamental integrity of the person or system from harmful encroachment. Therefore, in all cases where an individual or system is concerned, boundaries must be sufficiently well-defined for healthy functioning.

Disadvantages of closed/rigid boundaries in families

- ♥ Decreased flexibility/adaptability
- ♥ Absolute sub-ordinance
- ♥ Increased limitations
- ♥ Rules are absolute/immutable
- ♥ Creation of isolation
- ♥ Emotional needs not fulfilled
- ♥ Disorganization
- ♥ Disengagement (little interaction)
- ♥ Confusion
- ♥ No sense of connection

Disadvantages of open/diffuse boundaries in families

- ♥ Enmeshment (emotional over-involvement)
- ♥ Decreased autonomy
- ♥ No rules
- ♥ Decreased privacy
- ♥ Disorganization
- ♥ Overindulgence
- ♥ Confusion
- ♥ Regressive behaviors
- ♥ Decreased personal growth
- ♥ Clinginess
- ♥ Decreased self-confidence

Advantages to having well-defined, clear boundaries in families

- ♥ Autonomy
- ♥ Adaptability/flexibility
- ♥ Healthy interdependence
- ♥ Individual emotional safety
- ♥ Assertiveness
- ♥ Resourcefulness
- ♥ Organization
- ♥ Resiliency
- ♥ Closeness with individuality protected
- ♥ Connectedness
- ♥ Efficiency
- ♥ Healthy self-esteem
- ♥ Emotional needs fulfilled
- ♥ Self-confidence
- ♥ Respect for privacy

Families are considered closed systems when they construct rigid boundaries, thus shutting themselves off from positive external input or interaction, as well as negative. This creates stagnation, regression, and disorganization within the system. On the other hand, if the family keeps itself open (not diffuse) to outside input, but with well-defined individual and family boundaries, they are more likely to be resilient in the face of trials and crises. These families are more adaptable, organized, and open to new experiences, rather than being stuck in behavioral patterns that do not work.

Reflection

"Before I built a wall, I'd ask to know
what I was walling in or walling out."
-Robert Frost

Families who utilize all the resources they have are more likely to be resilient. It does not matter whether your family is a blended family, an intact family, or a single parent household. The key is to respect individual differences between members, such as personality/temperament style, understand individual roles, and respect and seek to fulfill individual needs. If expectations within your family are realistic, boundaries clear, and communication kept open, then your family will be able to weather the storms that cross your familial territory and you will be able to develop strategies to solve problems successfully.

In table 1, you can see the difference between interacting with unclear boundaries vs. clear boundaries. Notice the nuances between each way of functioning that most people innately know to be true, but often do not adhere to as much as they intend.

Table Differences between interacting with unclear boundaries and clear (intact) boundaries

Unclear boundaries	Clear boundaries
Compromising and complying as you make exceptions for others. Doing things for others because you cannot say "No."	Negotiating while keeping your values intact. Saying "No" when necessary and only doing favors that you choose to do.
Allowing yourself to be manipulated by flattery.	Distinguishing genuine compliments and feedback from manipulation.
Viewing others as the cause of your positive or negative feelings and relinquishing responsibility.	Viewing others as stimulating your feelings, but taking responsibility for them yourself.
Consistently doing more and more for less fulfillment or compensation.	When what you do procures results, you do more, if possible.
Not allowing yourself to feel angry and remaining only hurt and victimized.	Acknowledging all feelings (and expressing them appropriately), including pain and anger.
Altering your plans, thoughts, feelings, and behaviors, for another's benefit; disregarding intuition and personal limits.	Acknowledging others' circumstances while staying focused on your own needs; honoring intuition and personal integrity.
Allowing yourself to ruminate and obsess about someone else.	Allowing yourself to be affected by another, while staying focused on your own needs.
Allowing your thoughts, feelings, and space to be an open book.	Protect your privacy and secrets without having to fabricate stories.
Focusing mainly on others' needs, rather than taking time for yourself.	Utilizing self-care behaviors by engaging in hobbies or activities that you enjoy.
Trying to get close to another who only cares for his or her own needs.	Nourishing intimacy with only those who can extend reciprocal love and acceptance.
Allowing another to abuse you or your children, emotionally or physically.	Insisting that you and others around you have safe boundaries.

Parental Roles

It is important to remember that the job of parenting your children is the most challenging and probably the most difficult job that any of you will ever undertake. However, the roles of parents change over time in respect to the age of the child and his or her stage of development. Consider, for instance, that the parent is no longer the dominant force in the adolescent's life, but rather takes on the role of director and advisor.

When your child is an infant it is your job to take care of *every* element of his or her being, physical, emotional, and relational. As children grow through toddlerhood you continue to manage nearly every aspect of their lives while allowing them to investigate through curiosity, discovery, and risk taking. You are still the caretaker and nurturer of their physical and emotional needs. You are their playmate, guide, and their safety net. As they make mistakes and learn from them, they build their autonomy, which becomes the foundation of their authentic self.

As your child begins to socialize with peers in school and in sports or other activities, you are no longer managing every moment of their life. To some extent, you are letting them go. You help guide them through life as they discover new tasks, interaction skills, activities, and gender identity. This is the age when you can witness your children's blossoming gifts and help them to build their authentic selves as they venture into uncharted territory in the outside world. You remain their teacher, counselor, and moral guide as they experience hardship and failure. Until adolescence, you as a parent play the biggest part in your child's life.

Once children become teens however, your role in their lives minimize drastically. You are no longer a micro-manager of every facet of their life, but a director, who, like in the theater, gives them ideas and helps them to play their roles on the stage of life while allowing them the freedom to experiment, practice, and perfect their place in the world, through the making of mistakes. You need to respect their unique abilities to make decisions for themselves and

have input about what they do. Otherwise they may feel inade
frustrated, stifled, and become resistant or rebellious.

You may be running the show on the big issues, but teenagers need the opportunity to create their own identity and life. They make mistakes and you pick them up by supporting and guiding them, as well as giving them the chance to try again. This is how you allow your teenager to discover his or her authentic self.

Remember

You are growing up alongside your child.

From day one of your child's birth, you are raising an adult, so pay attention to your roles and how they change, in order to allow your child to successfully fill his or her own roles. Nurturance for your child must be an ever-present thread interweaving itself through each developmental stage. You are the one with the charge of fulfilling your children's needs continuously throughout their growth process.

Therefore, the quality of your parenting depends largely on the quality of your relationship with yourself and others. Having clear boundaries, a strong healthy family structure, and understanding your role as a parent, makes the immense job of raising emotionally healthy children, come naturally.

Do not forget, if you have teenagers, there is a good likelihood that you are chronologically in a stage where you have a lot of changes taking place in your own life, as well as your teen does. For instance, your own parents may be elderly and need additional care or you may be reaching or are currently in menopause. These occurrences add to the stress you may encounter during your child's adolescence. Your authenticity and attention to changes that occur in yourself, your family, and your children plays a huge role in how your children will define themselves as they grow.

It is not too late to start making positive changes in your family system that will benefit your entire family over time. Start now by setting clear boundaries for yourself, examining the hierarchy in your family, and establishing solid roles for the adults and children in your family. You are setting the stage for healthy growth by taking action and analyzing potential problem areas. Take into account your own stage of development and consider how that is affecting your family. By honestly taking responsibility for your roles and examining your family structure you will strengthen those ties that bind.

Questions to Consider

1. Contemplating the developmental stage that your child is currently in, which roles do you successfully fulfill as a parent?
2. Which aspects of your parental roles could you improve upon?
3. Where are you at developmentally in your life? How are your transitions affecting your role as a parent?

Chapter 4

Speaking the Truth

"It takes two to speak the truth,
—one to speak, and another to hear."
-Henry David Thoreau

All behavior is communication. Relationships, both positive and negative, are 100% communication. Even silence is a form of communication. Specifically, we are concerned in this book with the types of communication that parents use with their children. Because communication is so vitally important, it can renew or destroy relationships. In respect to children, their experience of you as a parent begins and ends with the way you communicate with them, either deliberately or inadvertently.

It is also important to remember that adults more often communicate verbally while children tend to communicate physically. For instance, when children act out through misbehavior it is an attempt on their part to communicate something. Parents must learn then to communicate physically (e.g., a pat on the back or touch on the shoulder), as well as verbally, in order for children to feel as if they are being heard. The younger the child is, the more important the physical contact with him or her.

During specific developmental stages, parents must pay attention to distinct aspects of how they communicate. These stages and communication behaviors follow:

Infant/Toddler: Pay attention to your volume, tone of voice, body language, rhythm, using a small number of words, eye contact, and getting down to your child's level; keep it simple! *Remember your main roles here are as guardian and nurturer.*

School-age: Pay attention to your volume, tone of voice, body language, active listening, and the child's new increase in attention span. Engage your child in conversation, but still keep commands and directions simple! Encourage feeling words and begin to teach "I" statements. *Remember your main role here is to guide.*

Adolescence: Pay attention to your volume, tone of voice, and body language. Avoid lecturing, nagging, and arguing. Ask open-ended questions to engage adolescents in conversation and learn to negotiate. Summarize what they say for clarification, stay in control, make an appointment for the important stuff, and keep it brief! Don't forget to breathe! *Remember your main role here is to direct.*

When communicating with your child, it is imperative that you are genuinely interested in what they have to say, as well as being sincere with your words. As you practice authenticity, your communication must remain non-threatening, non-judgmental, and above all, honest. It is your job to model this healthy communication to your children helping them to learn critical thinking skills, to make valuable moral judgments, and to maintain personal significance.

With adolescents especially, do not force the verbal communication process. Learn to be quiet and give them a chance to talk at their own pace. Try making a date with your adolescent for the big issues. When you have an attitude of respect and genuine interest in what your adolescent has to say, including opinions, disagreements, perceptions, wants, and needs, you will discover that he or she will be much more willing to have a collaborative discussion with you. In the coming pages, we will reiterate the importance of the gifts of effective communication and discuss examples of healthy expression and assertiveness.

Remember

Your children learn respect from you.
They are not born with the knowledge
of how to extend it, unless it's been modeled for them.

Effective communication includes a myriad of gifts of self-expression. As you have now learned, some parents are stronger in some gifts than they are in others, but the more consistently you use your own communication gifts, the more successful your interactions will be with your children. We provided explanations of communication gifts in chapter 1. We suggest you return to that chapter briefly to remind yourself of your potential strengths.

All of these communication gifts are essentially rolled-up into one major skill of healthy expression. This is the "I" Message. "I" messages are a form of communication which uses "I feel," "I think," or "I believe" statements, rather than "You" statements.

Example: "I feel hurt when you yell at me like that. I would prefer that you tell me calmly what you're upset about."

When used consistently the "I" message is a non-threatening way to remain assertive, yet maintain your own integrity and responsibility for feelings, thoughts, and behaviors. It is the most authentic form of communication. It avoids blaming, finger-pointing, accusing, and whining and the person you are communicating with is less likely to become defensive. On the other hand, if you use "You" statements, that person will likely perceive you as being attacking.

With this form of communication you are essentially stating only those things that you notice about a situation through your senses (i.e., visual, auditory, tactile, taste, & smell), what you think and feel about the situation, and what you need from the other person. You maintain personal integrity and are true to your emotions and thoughts as you remain self-aware and honest. Because you can only know your own thoughts, feelings, wishes, and needs, you are not trying to guess what the other person is trying to convey to you. Therefore, you are able to stay in the present moment.

Unless you express what you would like to be changed, you cannot realistically expect that change to take place. This is how you and your communication partner (e.g., child, spouse, co-worker, etc.) both get your needs fulfilled.

Remember

Always use your communication gifts
in conjunction with "I" messages.

As you utilize your gifts of effective communication, practice these "I" messages diligently when conversing with your children. Once you have a firm grasp on these concepts, you will learn to implement them within your own style of conveying an idea or asking for what you want or need.

Case Example

The following example describes a situation in which a mother uses some of her gifts as she communicates with her 12-year-old son:

Johnny brought home his report card to show his mother, throwing it on the kitchen table saying, "Here, I hope you're happy." He promptly stomped off to his bedroom.

His mother looked at the report card and noticed that Johnny received one B, two C's, two D's, and an F. She was upset, but she recognized that Johnny seemed even more upset (Attentiveness).

She walked down the hall to Johnny's bedroom and knocked on his door. When Johnny opened the door he was wiping tears from his cheek.

"It looks like you're pretty upset about this report card," his mother empathized. Johnny turned around and flopped himself face down on his bed, hitting his pillow with his fist and mumbling disappointment under his breath.

"I'll bet it's pretty frustrating to put in all that time and hard work and still not do as well as you would like," his mother said (Empathy; Engaging).

"I'm not frustrated," Johnny retorted. "I'm mad (Conversation is now open)!"

"Yeah, it looks like it. Can you tell me what you're so mad about (Active listening; Inquiry)?"

"It's not fair!" Johnny exclaimed. "My teachers don't like me."

"Is it possible," Johnny's mother asked, "that it's not so much the teachers? Do you think there could be another reason?"

"No."

"Have you been giving your teachers a hard time?"

"No!"

"Maybe you're struggling with some of the material presented in class. Did you complete all of your homework?"

"You don't know anything!" Johnny snapped. "Everybody's out to get me. You don't care! Just leave me alone."

"You know, Johnny, I feel hurt when you speak to me that way (Honesty; Self-control). I like for you to speak your mind. However, I would prefer that you don't attack me, but rather tell me how you're feeling and what you're thinking ("I" Message; Assertiveness). Now why don't we talk about this? Your grades have always been pretty good. What can I do to help (Availability; Openness)?"

"I hate this school!" Johnny yelled. "I'm failing everything. Nobody likes me. It's too hard."

"I knew it would be hard for you when we moved here (Understanding; Intuition). It's difficult going to new a school, meeting new friends, and middle school is much different than elementary school. It's a lot of change to get used to."

"It sucks," Jonnie whispered.

"I'll bet it does. I remember when my father got a new job and we had to move. It was really tough to leave all my friends and try to fit into a new school. I was pretty scared, too (Genuineness)."

"Yeah…but it's not fair."

"No, it's really not fair. It sounds like you're pretty angry about that too (Empathy)."

"Yeah, why did you make me move? Why do I have to go to this school?"

Johnny's mother discussed the purpose of their moving and how difficult it was for everyone, while empathizing with, rather than discounting, his feelings. She expressed many of her feelings too, her fears, sadness, and anger, in particular. She remained calm and as the discussion progressed, it was clear that Johnny's slipping grades had little to do with not understanding the work or even that he did not get along with his teachers. Johnny felt out of place and had difficulty making friends. He felt hopeless, useless, and like he was a failure.

Instead of telling Johnny that he needed to try harder or that failing was unacceptable, his mother showed love, respect, and caring for what he was going through. She explained to him that, "One 'F' is not the end of the world."

"But I only got one decent grade," Johnny said.

"Honey, I'm so proud of you. A failing grade does not mean you're a failure. You are special regardless of your grades. Maybe we can work together to figure out how to raise all the others. What are your thoughts as to how you can feel more a part of things? How can I help you handle this situation?"

They went on to find solutions to some of Johnny's difficulties, like getting him involved in extracurricular activities where he could find social success and achieve self-competence. You can see how his mother's use of her gifts of communication kept this situation from becoming overwhelming for the two of them. Through her authenticity she turned it into a learning experience for her son while further building their relationship.

It must be clarified that situations such as this one cannot work-out successfully if you do not first acknowledge your children's feelings. Acknowledging their feelings lets your children feel heard. It lets them know that you are listening and that you understand what your children are going through, so that they can begin finding their own solutions. It opens the conversation and lets them know that you care and that if they need your help, they can ask. Acknowledging your child's feelings is the foundation of good communication.

It is most important to focus your attention on which feelings may be difficult for you to recognize or accept in your children. For instance, if you think of the five foundational feelings that humans express—happiness, sadness, hurt, fear, and anger—parents can have a hard time dealing with their children's sadness (or crying). This emotion may make them feel vulnerable or perhaps they were not allowed to cry when they were children. Anger is another confusing expression, again due to the parent's own experience of this emotion or because it can immediately cause defenses to erupt.

The fact is everybody has a right to their natural emotions. It is the behavior tied to the emotion which may become troublesome. If some feelings are more difficult for you than others, then you will need to become aware of this and then draw from your gifts to help you improve your responses.

Remember

Acknowledging your children's feelings
helps them to build their authentic self,
from which communication
is honest & genuine.

Questions to Consider

1. Which feelings were okay for you to express when you were a child?
2. Which feelings were you not allowed or encouraged to express as a child?
3. Which of your children's feelings are difficult for you to deal with?
4. Which of your children's feelings are easier for you to deal with?

Negative Patterns of Communication

When you are not practicing your gifts and coming from a place of authentic strength, you are more likely to use negative patterns of communication which often become habit-forming. People are not usually taught healthy communication by their parents and the faulty patterns that are passed down through family generations can become entrenched in how they interact. Sometimes parents get lazy or impatient and speak before thinking. These patterns can create **power struggles** and **emotional meltdowns** with your children when you are not paying attention to what is really occurring within them. Common signs that your child is experiencing an emotional meltdown are crying or outward expressions of anger and defiance.

Additionally, yelling, criticism, and sarcasm are typical parental reactions to a child's defiance and oppositional behavior. Parents unfortunately can make statements that are destructive, rather than constructive, which do not address the emotional need that the child is experiencing and attempting to fulfill. Interactions, therefore, can get out of control when the parent does not master the art of disengagement. Thus, the negative or positive flow of communication is dependent on the parent's awareness and understanding of his or her own emotions, while attending to the child's emotions and needs.

Power Struggles and Meltdowns

Every parent knows what it is like to feel that he or she is at war with a child in a struggle to "win" each battle. When your child is attempting to engage in a power struggle, becoming defiant (or even aggressive), there is usually something occurring beneath the surface that has little or nothing to do with the situation at hand. There is often some level of frustration or anxiety that they are experiencing or some need that they perceive as not being fulfilled. This was the situation in the case example of Peggy and Jason in chapter 2. In these situations, something is bothering your child and it is your job as a parent to find out what it is, rather than engaging him or her in a power struggle or unwittingly encouraging their meltdowns.

When you are in a public place during one of these power struggles and are merely concerned with what others think of you, then you are not being authentic and using your strengths and you will inevitably have regrets later. For example, one common problem that parents encounter with young children is the perpetual temper tantrum in the grocery store. If the parent continues to give the temper tantrum attention and battle with the child or allow this behavior to continue simply because the parent has already spent valuable time shopping, then the child will learn nothing from the experience and is destined to repeat the behavior. However, if the parent leaves the shopping cart (even if he or she is already at the checkout stand) and removes the child from the store, the child will learn that such behavior will not have its desired effect. Parents, who respond in this way, refuse to be embarrassed or to forfeit the authority over their child, maintaining their own and their child's integrity.

Avoiding Potential Power Struggles

Decipher; **I**ntuition; **S**urface; **E**mpathy; **N**otice	**G**ifts; **A**ction	**G**enuineness; **E**ducation
Using your gifts of empathy, intuition, and active listening, try to understand what is really occurring under the surface for your child—beneath the behavior being manifested. Acknowledge your child's feelings and then decide if the situation is really worth struggling over.	Use all of your personal gifts to interact with your child as you decide what your next course of action will be.	Remain authentic and respond in a way that fulfills your child's needs while making the situation a learning experience for him or her.

Note: Notice the acronym "DISENGAGE" to help you understand the necessary steps to consider in a power struggle situation.

Avoiding potential power struggles

Remember

Practice makes *almost* perfect.

Once you have navigated your way through your child's

meltdown, deal with the situation modeling calmness. If need be, do some deep breathing and counting with your child to naturally calm yourself and your child physiologically. If it is not possible to have a discussion immediately following the incident, then come back to it later when you are both in a better emotional position to do so.

As the two of you explore the situation, discuss ways in the future that your child can become aware of his or her anger before it becomes overwhelming, such as noticing physical signs. Examples of these may be tightness in their chest, clenched fists, trembling, headache, feeling flush, clenching teeth, or shallow breathing. Teach your children self-talk, as well. Help them learn to tell themselves that they can be calm, that they can handle their emotions without losing control.

You and your child need to discuss ways to show anger without hurting him or herself or another person. Suggest that your child discover another outlet for his or her feelings, such as listening to his or her favorite music, finding a special cooling-down place that feels safe, or doing deep breathing exercises. For younger children, suggest that they draw a picture of their anger or write down what they are angry about. In fact teaching your children to journal can be a healthy lesson that can carry them through many parts of adolescence and even adulthood.

Remember
When you get into power struggles with your child,
nobody benefits!

Common Traps in Communication

When communicating with anyone, especially your children, it is important to avoid the most common communication traps. It is actually fairly common for most of us to engage in unhealthy, mistaken communication patterns and utilize cognitive distortions within our interactions. Because we are not taught healthy communication as children, we must make an effort to learn it as an adult.

When people do not pursue healthy, assertive communication, they frequently utilize passively or actively aggressive expressions such as silence, blaming, criticizing, judging, or attacking others with their own definitions of reality. They discount and reject others, setting up power struggles, closing channels of healthy communication, and depleting their own and the other person's energy and integrity. This allows avoidance of responsibility for their statements and sets up a pattern of shame-based thoughts, feelings, and behaviors, closing all options for further communication.

The following are communication traps which become episodic limitations when you are not using your gifts:

1. **All-or-nothing thinking:** Things are seen by dichotomous, black and white standards with no gray area.

Example: "Everyone knows how to do that." Or, "Good kids don't act that way."

♥ The way to counteract all-or-nothing thinking is by using the gift of *Genuineness.*

2. **Blaming & Accusing:** Refusing to take responsibility and focusing on someone else as the source of your negative feelings.

Example: "If you wouldn't have taken so long, I wouldn't have been late."

♥ The way to counteract blaming and accusing is by using the gift of *Respect.*

3. **Catastrophizing:** Believing that whatever happens is so terrible or traumatic that you will never be able to move beyond it.

Example: "I can't believe you disobeyed your teacher! You're probably going to fail now."

♥ The way to counteract catastrophizing is by using the gift of *Calmness.*

4. **Defensiveness:** Defending, making excuses, or retaliating when perceiving yourself as being threatened, attacked, or criticized.
    Example: "You're upset because I missed your game? Do you have any idea what kind of day I've had at work?"
    ♥ The way to counteract defensiveness is by using the gift of *Honesty*.

5. **Hopelessness:** Seeing only the negatives in life and refusing to acknowledge the positives.
    Example: "Nothing is ever going to change."
    ♥ The way to counteract hopelessness is by using the gift of *Faith*.

6. **Jumping to Conclusions:** Assuming you know the details of the situation without bothering to inquire.
    Example: "You probably hit the other boy first. Otherwise you wouldn't have gotten in trouble."
    ♥ The way to counteract jumping to conclusions is by using the gift of *Empathy*.

7. **Lecturing & Moralizing:** Giving too much attention to an issue while detracting from its original intent thereby decreasing the impact of the message.
    Example: "Bla, bla, bla, bla, bla." (This is what your children hear).
    ♥ The way to counteract lecturing and moralizing is by using the gift of *Active listening*.

8. **Martyrdom statements:** Playing the victim role.
    Example: "You never do anything for me."
    ♥ The way to counteract martyrdom statements is by using the gift of *Compassion*.

9. **Mind-reading:** Assuming what others are thinking, regardless of having insufficient evidence of their thoughts.

Example: "You think I'm lazy and that I don't care."

♥ The way to counteract mind-reading is by using the gifts of *Inquiry & Understanding*.

10. **Name-calling & Labeling:** Assigning negative traits to another person.

Example: "You can't even pick-up after yourself. You're such a lazy slob."

♥ The way to counteract name-calling and labeling is by using the gift of *Compassion*.

11. **Over-generalization:** Judging a single incident by global terms, making it much bigger than it is in reality.

Example: "You never do your chores."

♥ The way to counteract over-generalization is by using the gift of *Honesty*.

12. **Passive aggressiveness:** Indirect, dishonest, and inhibited form of aggression that displaces feelings and is both self and other denying.

Example: Giving someone the silent treatment.

♥ The way to counteract passive aggressiveness is by using the gifts of *Attentiveness* and *Genuineness*.

13. **Negative Prophecy:** Predicting a negative future.

Example: "You'll never get anywhere with an attitude like that." Or "You'll never succeed in life with those kinds of grades."

♥ The way to counteract prophecy is by using the gift of *Wisdom*.

14. **Should statements:** Interpreting things by some unrealistic standard, instead of focusing on what really is, implying failure without compliance.

Example: "You should be able to get better grades than that."

♥ The way to counteract should statements is by using the gift of *Teaching & Understanding*.

15. **Threats:** Using intimidation to get what you want.

Example: "If you can't keep your things picked up, I'm going to get rid of all your toys."

♥ The way to counteract threats is by using the gift of *Clarity & Directness*.

16. **Comparisons:** Focusing on others or events when interpreting another's behavior in terms of unrealistic standards.

Example: "Why can't you get good grades like your brother?"

♥ The way to counteract comparisons is by using the gift of *Compassion*.

As you can see, the traps of communication are numerous, as are the gifts. It is important to remember that individuals communicate in different ways. There are some parents whose eloquence and tenderness can make a lecture feel like a "good talk" to a child. There are other parents whose communication gifts are less wordy; like a certain look or a hug that speaks volumes to the child who receives it. While communication can take many forms however, the result should remain the same, sharing your authentic self with your children, regardless of the situation.

Reflection

"You can discover more
about a person in an hour of play
than in a year of conversation."
-Plato

The "how" is inevitably more important to a child than the "what" in communication. So pay attention to your body language, your tone of voice, and your proximity to the child when communicating with him or her. Old habits die hard. Patterns of communication are learned over time and are not easily undone. If you are rushed, stressed, tired, or angry, those old patterns may resurface. Take your time, pay attention, and watch the signals from your child. They will notice a change in the way you communicate and eventually will model this positive change in their own style.

Questions to Consider

1. What are your communication gifts/strengths?
2. What common communication traps do you fall into?
3. What negative patterns of communication would you like to work on?
4. How do you currently deal with meltdowns?

Chapter 5

Laying the Foundation

"Self-respect is the fruit of self-discipline;
the sense of dignity grows with the ability to say no to oneself."
-Abraham J. Heschel

In this chapter we will be discussing the underlying elements of discipline and the importance of laying a strong and enduring foundation. It is necessary to understand your own childhood and how you were parented when assessing your own parenting style. It is also essential to examine the function of misbehavior and the "why" underneath your children's actions. This understanding will lead you discernibly into gaining insight into your own values and building a plan for discipline that is grounded in wisdom and values. Authentically speaking, unraveling your own defenses will help you to better understand your children and your responses to their behavior.

The word discipline comes from the Latin word, *disciple,* which means a follower of truth and principle, or an honorable leader. But in order to fulfill this meaning, children must have models of truth, principle, and honorable behavior. You are their model.

A Brief History of Discipline

Many people refer to the "good old days" when children obeyed their parents without question. Unfortunately, they also thought children should be seen and not heard. However, these so-called "good-old-days" were a time when wives modeled submission to their husbands, husbands modeled submission to their employers, and most of them modeled submission to God. Children worked alongside their parents and were needed for economic survival. Personal and family responsibility was valued. Although ideas about how to function within the family could have seen improvement "back then," there is much we can learn from the examples set by our predecessors.

Today, with the many societal changes we have experienced, these values have changed. Apparently, these changes are what society calls progress. Submission is no longer modeled, childhood is considered merely a developmental stage, and children are indulged in the name of love without any effort or investment on their part.

Life skills and responsibility training are simply neglected because of busy lifestyles or a lack of understanding of the importance of children's contributions. It is important to understand that children develop responsibility when they are given the opportunity to learn in an atmosphere of kindness, firmness, dignity, and respect. They do not develop responsibility when parents are too strict and controlling or when they are too permissive.

Remember

Display of responsibility should be in
direct relation to the extension of privilege.

Questions to Consider

1. Were your parents too strict, too permissive, or somewhere in the middle?
2. Was personal and family responsibility part of your upbringing?
3. How do you teach your children responsibility and values?

Parenting Styles and Their Effects on Children

Reflection

"Liberty without obedience is confusion.
Obedience without liberty is slavery."
-William Penn

There are five main types of parents, Authoritarian, Indulgent, Permissive, Neglectful/Abusive, and Authoritative. The most common type of parent that many of us were raised by is the **Authoritarian**. This type of parent is generally strict and focused on excessive control. This is the parent who believes in *obedience without liberty*, for their children to "do as I say, not as I do," and allows few choices on their children's part. When their children ask why they must do what they are told this parent simply responds with, "Do it because I said so."

The type of parent which is quickly becoming today's standard is the **Indulgent** parent. In a society that is becoming extremely materialistic, fast-paced, over-stressed, and over-worked, indulgent parents are becoming the norm. They are over-compensating and often guilt-driven, basically telling their children, "You can have whatever you want, as long as you stay out of my hair, make me look good, and behave in a socially acceptable manner."

This teaches children to be concerned with what everyone else thinks, rather than realizing their own intrinsic worth. Feelings become meaningless and merely a means to an end. Children come to believe, *my parents don't have time for me, so they buy me stuff.* Or, *I am only worthy when I am getting something from my parents.*

Reflection

"The thing that impresses me most about America
is the way parents obey their children."
-King Edward VIII

Children feel the only way to achieve belonging and significance then is by manipulating other people into their service. They grow up lacking a work ethic, feeling entitled, and believing that the world owes them a living. They also tend to behave with little responsibility and hold themselves accountable for almost nothing.

Sometimes a component of over-protectiveness exists with indulgent parents, which often stems from some pain in the parent's past or even problems during or shortly after childbirth, creating anxiety over their child's well-being—fear gone awry. Children who are raised in this way however, are not given the opportunity to make mistakes that they can learn from and therefore, do not learn resilience and self-confidence. They grow up not learning the life skills necessary to live in the world successfully.

Remember

Raising children is like
nurturing a flower from a seedling
to a mature and resilient blossom.

Similar to the indulgent parent is the **Permissive** parent. Essentially, these parents believe in *liberty without obedience* and teach their children few to no limits. They give their children unlimited choices and are basically saying, "Do whatever you want." Without structure and limits, children with this type of parent have boundaries that are too open and unclear, making it difficult to know where they end and others begin. Although adolescents with a permissive parent will claim that their mom or dad is the coolest because they let them do anything, they secretly feel uncared for as a result of no limits.

Unfortunately, there have always been and probably always will be neglectful or abusive parents. **Neglectful** parents do not meet their children's physical, emotional, or spiritual needs. These parents are wholly unavailable and essentially come from a perspective of, "I don't care. I just can't deal with you, or your feelings/emotions." This may be the worst parent a child can have because he or she is extremely lonely in the resulting solitude, have difficulty learning appropriate social skills, and often feel utterly empty. These children frequently become hopeless and have a limited drive to even attempt to achieve or succeed.

Abusive parents may inflict pain physically, emotionally, verbally, or sexually. Abuse in these families may in fact involve all of these. Parents with this type of debase behavior are often unpredictable and are essentially telling their children, "Stay out of my way or I will hurt you." Children with abusive parents often come to believe that they should give up because there is not much they can do that does not invite shame and pain. They spend a great deal of energy in acquiring rebellion and avoidance skills. As adults they may become abusers themselves or victims of abuse.

Authoritative parenting is what we are aiming for in this book. This type of parenting is concerned with *liberty with obedience*. Authoritative parents focus on positive discipline designed to teach, give their children choices with limits, and model respect. That is they believe *you can choose within limits that show respect for all.* They concentrate on opening channels of communication with their children, are genuine and real with their children, and allow their children to make mistakes they can learn from. These parents can also be honest about their own mistakes without compromising their authority. By being firm with dignity and respect, they teach their children critical thinking, self-assuredness, and empathy for others. The authoritative parent is the ultimate epitome of an authentic parent.

It is important that you discover what type of parent you are through the awareness of what type of parent you had as a child. Since there are usually differences between you and your child's other parent as to parenting styles, understanding from which perspective each of you is coming is essential to good parenting. Somewhere on the spectrum of parenting types the two of you must meet and present a unified front in dealing with your children. Be willing to compromise for the benefit of your children while remaining true to your own values. It is imperative that you answer the question we asked in chapter 1, "Who do you want to be?"

Questions to Consider

1. Which type of parent were your mother and/or father? How did this affect you?
2. What type of parent are you now? How does your child respond to this type of parenting?
3. Which gifts can you draw from to work toward being a more authoritative, authentic parent?

Designing Discipline

Every discipline situation can be broken down into three parts, **expectations**, **compliance**, and **consequences**. When there are misbehavior or discipline issues, it means that there has been a breakdown in the understanding of and commitment to one of these three elements.

♥ **Expectations** are the implicit or explicit messages sent from parent to child regarding behavior. They can be developmentally appropriate, too high, or too low.

♥ **Compliance** is the child's behavior in response to the expectation. It can either fulfill or not fulfill the expectation of the parent.

♥ **Consequences** are the results of compliance or non-compliance. They can be natural, logical, punitive, or non-existent.

Heeding these elements of effective discipline creates self-discipline in your child and leaves his or her self-esteem intact. It works no matter what developmental stage your child is in or what stage you are in with your child. It is never too late to begin effective discipline techniques and you will inevitably notice first, negative and eventually, positive changes in their behavior.

The goal is always to make your expectations absolutely clear and developmentally appropriate. Then there can be no room for argument and your children are not confused about what direction they are to move in. Explicit and reasonable expectations lead to a higher rate of compliance from children which then results in positive consequences.

The downside is that breakdown occurs when parents fail to make their expectations clear or mismatch them with their child's level of development. This can occur when parents have not taken the time to explain their values to their children, are wishy-washy or unpredictable about what they expect, or have extremely different hopes than the other parent. Children caught between these differences are then confused and begin to test their parents with non-compliance which of course, results in negative consequences.

Short-term outcomes of using effective discipline techniques:

♥ Increased calmness (possible)—less chaos results in calmer children, increasing healthier behaviors such as more sleep
♥ Increased anxiety (possible)—change can produce anxiety because it is new and unfamiliar
♥ Exaggerated misbehavior because change causes a child to attempt to maintain the family system's balance

Long-term outcomes of using effective discipline techniques:

♥ Leveling off of exaggerated misbehavior
♥ Testing of the new limits and structure
♥ Longer term of leveling off
♥ Motivation to change behavior permanently

Motivations Underlying Your Child's Misbehavior

First things first—*expect* your children to misbehave. Testing is natural. It is what they are good at and it comes with the make-up of being a child. Some children fulfill this natural obligation more than others, some fulfill it less. It is nevertheless, their job and it always has its place. Its reasons may be related to you and your own chaos and it is undeniably an attempt to fulfill some need for them. It is your job to discover misbehavior's unique purpose, understand the underlying issues, and to discipline your child immediately and consistently. Notice the cognitive and emotional layers that can be present in these motivations in tables 3, 4, and 5.

Table Motivation of Acceptance: Thoughts, feelings, and reactions underlying misbehavior and leading to common problematic interaction patterns.

Example: Child seems to need constant attention.

Child's Distorted Thought	"I belong only when I am accepted and have your attention".
Child's Feeling	Lonely, hurt, sad, and/or ashamed.
Parent's Thought	"You're annoying me. You need to learn to take care of yourself because I can't always be there."
Parent's Feeling	Angry, frustrated, and/or irritated.
Parent's Reaction	Tendency to remind, punish, or reward with negative attention.
Child's Response to Parent's Reaction	Misbehavior will be reduced, but will likely return later.
Alternative Response for Parents	Be generous with positive attention. Acknowledge need for acceptance through open communication and redirect child's behavior. When no destruction of person or property, ignore misbehavior when possible.

Motivation of acceptance

Motivation of Control: Thoughts, feelings, and reactions underlying misbehavior and leading to common problematic interraction patterns.

Example: Child is engaging in a power struggle.

Child's Distorted Thought	"I belong only when I am winning or am in charge".
Child's Feeling	Stressed, anxious, scared, and/or out of control.
Parent's Thought	"I am the parent. You must do what I say. I will not put up with disobedience."
Parent's Feeling	Angry, threatened, and/or out of control.
Parent's Reaction	Engage in power struggle.
Child's Response to Parent's Reaction	Active-aggression or child submits with defiant compliance.
Alternative Response for Parents	Identify source of power struggle through empathy, open communication, and seek cooperative solution with the child.

Motivation of control

Motivation of Security: Thoughts, feelings, and reactions underlying misbehavior and leading to common problemtatic interraction patterns.

Example: Child lashes out (vengeance) or plays the victim (martyrdom).

Child's Distorted Thought	"I don't belong, so nothing matters."
Child's Feeling	Anger or hopeless/helpless.
Parent's Thought	"I don't understand why my child would want to hurt me. I must have done something wrong (or "What's wrong with him or her)."
Parent's Feeling	Deeply hurt or frustration & hopelessness.
Parent's Reaction	Retaliate, withdraw, or over-compensate through pity.
Child's Response to Parent's Reaction	Responds with defiance or helplessness. May seek revenge, withdraw, be passive-aggressive, or choose another form of misbehavior.
Alternative Response for Parents	Address situation through empathy, genuineness, and respect, & resolving any conflict through open communication. Set realistic expectations, encourage, & focus on strengths. Model perseverance.

Motivation of security

As you can see, the motivations behind your children's misbehavior are linked to their emotional needs and the fulfillment or non-fulfillment of these needs. Working to understand these motivations and learning to identify them is invaluable to effective, learning-based discipline. It can also awaken you to certain manifestations of your own life stressors that may be affecting your children. Once you identify these components of your child's misbehavior, you are more capable of making constructive changes for the betterment of your family.

Remember

When children are consistently motivated
by their unfulfilled needs
for acceptance, control, and security,
they do not develop the skills they need
to become authentic people.

Essentially, mastering the elements of discipline is at the root of understanding your child's behavior. Your expectations can make the difference in how your child responds to situations even when you are not around. Compliance is a choice that the child makes and consequences are external responses to that choice by the parent.

Evaluate your expectations. Make sure that they are appropriate for your child's age and developmental stage. Acknowledge your child's developmental achievements and level of responsibility before assigning expectations and privileges. Make your expectations as clear and explicit as possible. It can make a world of difference to genuinely share with your children exactly what is expected of them. The results are better behavior, clearer boundaries, and a more positive relationship with your children.

Questions to Consider

1. What are your expectations of your child? Are these expectations clear to your child?
2. What current discipline issues are you encountering?
3. How do you execute consequences? Are you consistent?
4. What is your child's motivation for his or her misbehavior? Do you see repeated patterns in his or her misbehavior?

Chapter 6

Calming the Storm

"There are some things you learn best in calm, and some in storm."
-Willa Cather

Principles of Natural and Logical Consequences

Now that you understand how discipline works, what your own style is, and the reasons why children misbehave, it is time to start building a plan. The goal of course, is still to remain authentic, not to mimic someone else's "miracle" cure. You know your children better than anyone else does. You were chosen just for them. Basing your discipline plan, then, on your own intrinsic family values, is the most natural method for raising emotionally healthy children.

This chapter is about creating harmony and peace in what may currently be a battleground between children and parents. Things have to make sense to be effective, so make sure you spend the time and do the work involved to get your household under control. If you want your children to grow in a healthy environment, then it is your responsibility to create it. Immerse them in love; however, do not let the little problems become severe issues.

When you do things for children that they can do for themselves, you are robbing them of the chance to develop self-respect, self-confidence, and a sense of accountability. Therefore, it is important for children to learn to be responsible for their own behavior and decisions. Simple rewards and punishment are merely external methods of changing children's behavior and are designed to either increase or decrease a specific behavior. They do not teach self-discipline and they deny children the opportunity to be responsible.

On the other hand, natural and logical consequences require children to be responsible for their own behavior. While utilizing these during the course of discipline, be both firm and kind. Firmness refers to your follow-through behavior, whereas kindness refers to the manner in which you present the choice. In general, talk less and act more.

Natural consequences

Natural consequences are those which permit children to learn from the fundamental order of the physical world. Look at the following examples:

1. If your child chooses not to bathe, then he or she will smell (increasing the likelihood of receiving negative remarks from friends).
2. If your child chooses not to go to bed on time, then he or she will be tired the next day and unable to complete necessary projects (which may bring further consequences).
3. If your child chooses to go out in cold weather without wearing a jacket, then he or she will get cold.
4. If your child chooses not to be on time for dinner, then it will be cold when he or she arrives at the table.

Logical consequences

Logical consequences are those which permit children to learn from the reality of the social order. For these consequences to be effective they must be reasonable and the child involved, must also see them as logical. Look at the following examples:

1. If your child does not do his or her schoolwork, then he or she is likely to have failing grades, or not get to participate in recess at school.
2. If your child does not complete his or her chores, then he or she gets no allowance or free time. There may also be additional chores added.
3. If your child fights about toys, then the toys are taken away.
4. If your child fights with his or her siblings, then he or she is placed in time-out (for separation purposes).
5. If your child chooses not to clean-up after him or herself, then free time is not allowed.
6. If your child chooses to break curfew, then you set and enforce an earlier curfew next time.
7. If your child breaks TV or phone rules, then privileges are suspended.

Ways to provide logical consequences

♥ Provide choices *acceptable* to you (e.g., "You can wear the red blouse or the white one."). Use a friendly tone of voice that communicates your goodwill and accept the child's decision. This makes sure the child is part of the solution, rather than the problem.

♥ Be consistent and firm with consequences, always following through. Leniency (i.e., giving in "just this once") discredits you and teaches your child to manipulate, creating a repetition of behavior. Always assure children that they may try again later.

♥ If the misbehavior is repeated, reapply the consequence and extend the time that must lapse before the child has the opportunity to try again.

The standard misbehavior that all children engage in is essentially mild. These are actions such as pouting, disobeying a request, or not finishing homework. When these behaviors go unchecked however, they can become habitual and increase in intensity, making them more severe in nature. Severe misbehavior falls into four basic categories. These are *cruelty, violence, destruction,* and *deception.*

Put simply, these severe misbehaviors cannot be tolerated and must be immediately addressed at the first sign, before they become habitual. All consequences for misbehavior must be appropriate, but as normal misbehavior becomes more severe, you will need to step-up the consequences. For example, while you may give your child a time-out for repeatedly interrupting you, hitting you would require at least a time-out, plus making amends (e.g., a written apology).

Remember

All consequences need to make sense
to your child in order to be effective.

Be patient, it will take time for natural and logical consequences to be effective and for you to learn how to apply them steadily. So practice, practice, practice!

Now that you have a better understanding of natural and logical consequences, it is important to discern the difference between punishment and discipline. Although punishment in some, rare instances may stop certain misbehavior, this cessation is based solely in a child's fear because they know what is unacceptable to their parents. However, it does not teach children how to make good decisions, how to control themselves, or be responsible for their own behavior when you are not around.

Therefore, punishment most often only stops the misbehavior in the short-term, while discipline has positive long-term effects. Keep in mind that punishment which includes grounding or suspension of privileges for *prolonged* periods of time, only serves to make your child angry, belligerent, or withdrawn. Simply put, consequences cannot be too severe. As you will see throughout this chapter, all discipline involves the implementation of natural and logical consequences. Table 6 outlines the differences between punishment and logical consequences (effective discipline).

Remember

Discipline does *not* equal punishment!!!

Table Results of implementing punishment vs. logical consequences

Punishment	Logical Consequences
Expresses the power of personal authority.	Express the impersonal reality of the social order.
Concentrates on exerting control.	Promotes self-control for all involved.
Rarely related to misbehavior.	Logically related to misbehavior.
Implies the child he or she is bad.	Imply no element of moral judgment.
Insists on obedience through fear.	Promotes obedience through logical reasoning.
Focuses on what is already past.	Are concerned with present and future behavior.
Associated with a threat, either open or concealed.	Are based on goodwill, rather than retaliation.
Demands obedience.	Permits choice.

Remember

"Let the punishment match the offense."

-Cicero

To reiterate, discipline does not equal punishment! Punishment does not teach self-discipline. Punishment succeeds in stopping misbehavior in the short term, however it will inevitably return. The long-term results of harsh punishment are resentment, revenge, rebellion, and retreat. Effective discipline is designed to teach and is a combination of clear-cut appropriate expectations, guidance towards compliance, and consistent, immediate natural or logical consequences.

The parent's goal in disciplining a child is to teach self-discipline in the parent's absence. If you discipline your children when they are young, adolescence will be more manageable and society will not have the disheartening task of disciplining them as adults. In addition, what you practice at home will play out in the real world. For example, if your children are taught to use manners at the dinner table, they will internalize this pattern and behave in public restaurants.

If discipline is taught with gentleness, directness, and consistency, it is not in and of itself, difficult. The work you put into it however, will dictate how much easier your job will become as your children grow. It is also directly proportional to the peace you will experience later.

The point is you must take action. If all of your discipline is based in verbal reprimands, you will find yourself becoming more and more exasperated. Not taking action leads to yelling, nagging, and general frustration if over-utilized and your children will be more likely to simply ignore you.

Remember

Your child deserves your dedicated
attention to good discipline.

Family Values

In order to develop a discipline plan utilizing family "rules" as the expectations for which discipline is based, you must begin with first understanding what *your* family values are. Once these are determined, you can better understand what rules your family can best function with.

It is important to know what your expectations are of your children, as well as yourself. For example, insisting your children make their beds every day is an unrealistic expectation, if you do not make yours. Therefore, this degree of tidiness would not be an important value for your family.

Remember
Expectations must be realistic.
Your child cannot reach standards
that are too high and they will not grow
if standards are too low.

There are major values which lay the foundation for who you want your children to be, such as treating others with kindness. However, there are also smaller minor values, such as cleaning up after yourself, which are aimed at teaching responsibility or making a household run more smoothly. Take a moment to think about some of the values that have importance to you. We have provided many examples of specific family values for your perusal. Maybe some of these fit for you, or perhaps you would like to reword them to fit your style, or maybe there are others that you can think of which are not on this list.

- ♥ Treat others with kindness and understanding
- ♥ Live life with integrity and be true to yourself
- ♥ Take responsibility seriously
- ♥ Sharing is a good way to make and keep friends
- ♥ Respect other people's property
- ♥ Teasing should be ignored
- ♥ Listen when someone is talking
- ♥ Recognize and understand what others are feeling
- ♥ Remember your manners
- ♥ Be patient, even when its hard
- ♥ Keep a positive attitude and try harder
- ♥ Keep your hands to yourself
- ♥ Show appreciation for the things others do for you
- ♥ Talk about what bothers you to people who are good listeners
- ♥ Stick up for yourself
- ♥ Don't be afraid to speak out
- ♥ Follow the rules; they are there for good reasons
- ♥ Set goals for yourself and work hard to achieve them
- ♥ Master the art of forgiveness
- ♥ Never give up
- ♥ Chores make the household run smoothly
- ♥ Cleanliness is important
- ♥ Education matters
- ♥ Work before play
- ♥ Family togetherness is important
- ♥ Do not lie, cheat, or steal

Remember
Authentic families are created
by authentic family values.

Once you have discovered what your values are, you can make a list of family rules based on these values. We have provided some examples for you of how to turn these values into rules, but you will need to come up with some of your own. Once you have created all of your family rules you can post them somewhere so that everyone in the family knows what they are. Make sure these rules are realistic or they will create problem situations within the family and will not hold up to the test of time. Do not forget the importance of these values and rules being the same for parents as they are for children (yes, you have rules and chores, too).

Remember
Never make a rule that is not
backed up by a value!

Family Rules

Examples:

♥ Rule—Do not take something that does not belong to you. This rule relates to the value that states one is to *"Respect other people's property,"* as well as, *"Do, not lie, cheat, or steal."*

♥ Rule—Complete your homework before going outside to play. This rule relates to the value of *"Work before play."*

♥ Rule—Everyone eats dinner together at the dinner table. This rule relates to the value of *"Family togetherness is important."*

Once you are able to visualize having minor values and major values, you can better understand how misbehavior can also be mild or severe. Therefore, once you have identified your family values and family rules you can begin to implement more clarified consequences for the rules which are broken, expectations that have not been met, and different degrees of misbehavior. As you implement these rules, of course, you may discover some that you had not previously thought of. If that is the case, merely add them to your list of rules, as long as they are in line with your family values.

Your values are the only things set in stone.

Remember
All consequences
must be implemented
immediately and consistently.

After you have completed your family rules you can design your specific discipline plan, charting common misbehaviors and their consequences for your children to see (see sample chart in Appendix B). By posting the chart you can always refer back to it if necessary, to remind your child of the respective consequences. You will then be able to implement individual and family chores.

Chores may need to be charted, as well, so that everyone knows what is expected of them (see sample chart in Appendix B). You might also want to increase compliance by rotating chores between children, so that they do not become easily bored with repeatedly performing the same task. Remember that every member of the family has chores, including parents. In fact, it is to your advantage for your children to see that you have chores too, so that they understand what it takes to run a household. Do not forget the importance of you recognizing your children's gifts and strengths, as well as their age and level of development when designing family rules, your discipline plan, and chores.

Remember
Discipline and chores
must be age appropriate.

It is essential to know that your approach to discipline sets the tone for your family's functioning. If you have no plan and therefore, merely discipline your children by the seat of your pants, you are creating an environment of chaos and your children will be negatively affected.

Discipline is most effective when it reflects the values of the family and is prescribed with love. You are teaching your children how to live now and in the future. Most likely, these lessons will be in some way passed on to the next generation. So, this is not a subject to be taken lightly. Discuss discipline with your spouse and your children as you develop your plan. Focus on solutions. Have a family meeting and work it out together. Expectations can be expressed clearly, chores can be a collaborative effort, and peace can be restored and maintained.

Questions to Consider

1. What is the atmosphere in your home?
2. How were you disciplined as a child?
3. Does your discipline style make sense to you and your children?
4. What would you like to change about your style of discipline?

Chapter 7

Running on Empty

"When we truly care for ourselves,
it becomes possible to care more profoundly
about other people. The more alert and sensitive we are to our
own needs, the more loving and generous we can be toward others."
-Eda LeShan

We thought it important to include a chapter in this book about the stressful lives each of us endure, because the feeling of being overwhelmed and "running on empty" has become commonplace and can be a profound detriment to exceptional parenting. Simply put, we live too hard. Most parents are overburdened and overscheduled. We do too much and we do it too fast. In today's society, more is better and time is money. Unfortunately, stress is the consequence and in excess is not only damaging to parenting, but to physical and emotional health, as well.

When we are stressed, our bodies, minds, and hearts are on overload. Our relationships suffer, our defenses rise up, and there is little time for reflection, relaxation, or rejuvenation. In regards to parenting, this kind of lifestyle is a set-up for disaster. Children get stressed-out too, especially when their parents are overwhelmed.

It is imperative that you become aware of the effects of stress on your family. Seriously consider taking a break and re-working your life. This is not a dress rehearsal. There are no trophies awarded at the end of the road to those who finish first or have the most stuff. There are however, multiple prizes throughout the life ahead of you if you take the time to acknowledge the wonders around you, to care for yourself and those you love, and appreciate what you have.

One of the most important pieces of your authentic parenting puzzle is the plan for designing your own life. You *can* stop being a victim of circumstance and a casualty of your own hectic schedule. How would you write the story of your life if you were its author? Consider the idea that you are, and as the designer, you have numerous choices and the ability to transform your entire life. Start small, work your way up, and don't forget to breathe.

Remember

Stress is harmful and damaging
to your health and your relationships.
It kills your authenticity by putting you on the defensive.
You are unable to use your gifts
if you are wound-up or depleted by stress.

Simplicity

Let's start with simplicity. You may be so used to being stressed-out that it might be uncomfortable to change things at first—to not perpetually be on "fast forward." The goal is to simplify your life enough so your authenticity can come shining through and allow you to be the parent you always wanted to be.

Simplicity is about cutting out the excess. Everything in your life that is not in some way benefiting you or your family can be put aside. Begin with your current schedule. Is your time and attention spread in several different directions? Do you always feel rushed? Are you burnt-out on your job? Do not hold back. Cut out everything for one week that is not absolutely necessary for survival. Go ahead, reschedule those commitments that drove you crazy anyway or just cross them off your schedule. The walls will not fall down around you if you do not attend every single meeting or event that takes place in your sphere of "commitments."

This may seem extreme at first, but it is absolutely necessary if you want to be an exceptional parent building authentic relationships with your children. Most children are overscheduled too and have little or no free time to play or daydream. Once you learn how to take back your life, you can give them back their childhood.

Remember

Cutting the excess is critical
to prioritizing your parenting.

Once you have taken these simple steps, you should notice immediately how much extra time you have. This is time that can be devoted to you and your family. Your personal growth and well-being are essential to your children's emotional health. You have probably heard the saying, "When momma's not happy, ain't nobody happy." The same goes for dads. The truth is that parents set the tone for the household. If that tone is stress and chaos, then the message received by the children is that life is confusing, hard, and cruel. They will wonder, *if they can't do it, how will I?*

After your week-long trial vacation from stress, look back and examine what you were able to do or not do with the extra time you afforded yourself. Analyze those commitments beyond work and home that drain your time and energy and decide their necessity. Then take a look at your work. Is it what you were meant to do or do you feel stuck? Does it fortify your authentic self? Are your children spending more time at the babysitter's or day-care than with you? Are you spending otherwise precious family time with people or on tasks that sap your energy and your resources? It is time to re-evaluate your outside friendships and activities. Relationships should be reciprocal and activities should be meaningful. If they are not, then they do not belong in your life.

Time-clutter

Time-clutter encompasses every moment in your life that does not benefit you and your family. Anything that wastes your time or takes away from your family qualifies as time-clutter. From the most basic morning rush-hour commute to someone tying up your time and attention on the telephone during dinner, time-clutter is everywhere.

Take a look at your calendar. How do you spend your average 24 hours? What can you permanently reduce or eliminate? Maybe your difficulty with clear boundaries makes it hard for you to say, "No," to certain requests. Look back to chapter 3 and reconsider which boundaries you can practice clarifying. When you begin to have doubt that you can actually simplify your life, contemplate the cost to your children of your being everywhere except with them.

Consider the possibility that a second job is not worth the time and effort if all it pays for is your day-care costs. Perhaps now is not the right time to go back to school. This does not mean it can never happen. Even volunteer work to help others, as great as your intentions are, can take a toll if you have nothing left to give to your family.

Try taking some time away from electronic devices, as well, such as television or the internet. Turn off your cell phone when you are home. These actions may be difficult at first, but well worth the effort. Without constant reliance on all of your modern conveniences—which by the way, serve to make your lives more hectic and complicated, and distract you from what is important (your family)—what will you be left with? The answer is simple—your children and more free time to play, daydream, rest, and build healthy relationships.

It is our belief that there is "time-clutter" in everyone's life. However, you do not get this time back with your children. Once you miss a milestone, it is gone, never to return. Your children are only little for a short time. They only say their first word, once. They only enter their first day of school, once. They only hit puberty, once (unfortunately, it can go on for some time, though). There are no "rollover minutes." Every moment is precious. If you are serious about creating balance and reducing stress, then do whatever it takes to make it work. The key is prioritizing.

Picture your ideal for you and your family. Is it material gain, or social success? Or, is it time to take walks with your children or read a good book? Hopefully, it is a manageable lifestyle that leaves room for appreciation, comfort, and intimacy, with the ability to help your children grow into healthy adults. They need you—the real you. They need your authentic presence most of all. Do not miss out on this opportunity. Be there. Be present with all of your wonder, excitement, warmth, and caring.

Reflection

"Out of clutter, find simplicity."
-Albert Einstein

Stuff-clutter

The next area to consider when undertaking simplicity is "stuff-clutter." Clutter creates stress. Order creates serenity. Serenity is the goal of simplicity and stress management. If you want peace in your life, then eliminate the clutter. Do some space clearing in your home (yes, every room), your car, and your work environment.

Research shows that children and adults are negatively affected by disorder. This is evidenced in classrooms and households where there is no serenity. Although children sadly can grow accustomed to it over time, their learning and creativity take on more energy in a calm and serene environment.

Involve your children in getting rid of what you do not need by tossing trash, donating outgrown or unused items, and organizing. This not only creates a more peaceful environment, it helps children learn valuable organizational skills, the giving of themselves in helping others, and control over their immediate space.

Think of all the time you waste searching for lost things. Consider the money wasted buying duplicates or the chaos created by disorder. Devote time every month or week to clutter control with your children and you will notice an immediate difference in the balance and energy flow in your home.

Streamlining

Fortunately, this exercise in simplicity is addictive. Streamlining your schedule and your stuff has instant benefits and gives you more time to focus and reflect on the important aspects of your life. The process of eliminating time and stuff-clutter helps kids and adults detach from material things and prioritize the important stuff.

The goal is to streamline your life in all areas. Instead of filling your voids with material goods and worthless activities, focus on what is important and create time to spend with your children.

Simplifying your life is a critical aspect of exceptional parenting. If your life is a mess, your children's will be too. Chaos is highly conducive to misbehavior, defiance, anxiety, and emotional meltdowns. Stressed-out parents inevitably make bad decisions, feel overwhelmed, and have difficult relationships with their children and significant others. So, make it a priority to prioritize! Your children deserve it. Do not miss out on their childhood because you are overscheduled. Forget about trying to figure out how to provide them with just "quality time" and give them quantity, as well as quality. Be available emotionally, physically, and spiritually. Play, sing, laugh, but get out of the fast lane. You cannot take care of your children when you are moving a hundred miles per hour, doing too much, and not taking care of yourself.

As you can see, stress-management and balance are absolutely essential to good parenting. We have provided a list of activities that can help reduce the stress of raising children and give parents a better chance at relating well to their children. Perhaps you can think of a few of your own.

Activities to reduce stress

- ♥ Rest
- ♥ Music
- ♥ Relaxation
- ♥ Crying
- ♥ Recreation
- ♥ Sex
- ♥ Exercise
- ♥ Humor
- ♥ Hobbies
- ♥ Spending time with close friends
- ♥ Support groups
- ♥ Psychotherapy
- ♥ Taking a bath
- ♥ Drinking hot cocoa and watching a good movie

Questions to Consider

1. In what areas of your life do you feel stressed?
2. What do you do when you are feeling overwhelmed?
3. How do you take care of yourself? Daily? Weekly? Monthly?
4. What can you eliminate (stuff or time-clutter) that is taking time away from your family or your sanity?

Chapter 8

Out of the Shadows

"Suffering is not a badge we need to wear proudly,
but a trophy to be merely remembered and placed on a shelf,
so that we may go on with the work of living triumphantly."
-J.D. DeForest

We include this chapter for the benefit of all those who live with old scars. You cannot move through life without having some, but you can learn to use your pain to enrich your life.

Wounds are inflicted when a person's emotional needs are not met. As children, it is difficult to express our needs and even more difficult to express our disappointment in their lack of fulfillment. When a child does not feel acceptance from a parent, for instance, he or she is wounded. If the parent does not give that child the opportunity to express his or her sadness, then that emotion is buried inside to fester until a later date.

As unexpressed wounds pile on top of one another this lack of communication becomes a habitual way of functioning which is carried into adulthood. The adult child can feel the same pain then from that parent as he or she continues to attempt to gain acceptance through the same means. When this acceptance is not extended it perpetuates the wound through a persistent lack of communication.

Healing Wounded Children

People can be wounded in countless ways, especially children. The younger they are, the more vulnerable they are. Each and every person has encountered pain in his or her life which can take many different forms. Some pain arises from everyday functioning at home such as, a parent yelling at a child, loneliness or disappointment caused by parents working a lot, or a scrape on the knee. These would be considered mild pains.

Others may be considered a higher, more moderate level of pain. They may include rejection from friends, failure at school, exclusion from peer activities, humiliation/embarrassment, or sibling rivalry.

Some wounds are created by more severe, traumatic occurrences. These may include the loss of a loved one, breakup of the family or divorce, fire in the home, drug or alcohol abuse by a parent, or a date rape of your teenager. Most damaging of course, is child abuse and neglect, which create wounds in children that can take a lifetime to heal. As a rule, the younger the child is when this takes place, the more devastating it can be.

These painful experiences can be opportunities for growth, but they must first be healed. We tend to want explanations for our suffering. We make incorrect interpretations about ourselves as children and carry these through life, especially in response to moderate and severe pain. Children often think they must be broken and they have to fix themselves.

If your child has been traumatized, then you have a special task ahead of you and you may need to seek professional help. In any event, healing pain of any kind requires love, compassion, warmth, gentleness, kindness, openness, and the desire to move through the healing process. So, listen to your children, tune into what they are experiencing, kiss their owies, and stay open to the possibility that some of their wounds may have been a direct or indirect result of your behavior.

Remember

"Any child who is hurt will
seek the comfort of loving parents."
-Wayne Muller, 1992

Children need to be noticed. Children must be able to experience feelings without the fear of hurting their parents or thinking that they are making their parents insecure. Your children need to develop trust for you, to feel secure in the expression of their true self. If there are problems in your child's social environment, you must counteract them with home and family. Your job is to protect, nurture, and care for their needs.

Help your children to learn to grieve their losses and pain without reprimanding them, laughing at them, making them feel weak, or minimizing the validity of their pain. Acknowledge their feelings and help them to move through the different stages of grief. Refuse to be blinded by denial and notice the warning signs that something is not right with your child. Be open to your child's questions, disagreements, choices, critical thinking, and mistakes.

Prescription for helping children heal

- ♥ Acknowledge their feelings and respect them (don't devalue)
- ♥ Do not pretend everything is fine
- ♥ Look for warning signs
- ♥ Make family problems the priority—not work problems or volunteering your time somewhere else
- ♥ Spend time with your children
- ♥ Provide outlets for sharing their pain
- ♥ Do not hide your family secrets
- ♥ Understand that children have unique gifts, too, and express themselves differently
- ♥ Be open to professional help

Healing Wounded Parents

The same rules apply for parents who have experienced pain, either in childhood or as adults. Pain is real and takes time to heal. An atmosphere of love and support is essential to all healing. If necessary, seek professional help for dealing with past hurts. At the very least, be kind to yourself and find someone to listen when you are ready to share your pain.

Resolving past issues and learning to move beyond the pain will help immensely in parenting your children and having a fulfilling life. Unfortunately, avoiding and not dealing with those past hurts will create problems, as parenting brings with it the feelings and problems that stir up old wounds. Sometimes children serve as reminders of your own pain and it is important not to have contempt for them and behave as to defend against them through angry aggression, avoidance, or rejection.

Reflection

"A house built out of self-betrayal
will sooner or later fall down and
mercilessly destroy human life—if not that of the builder,
then that of his children, who will sense the lie
without being aware of it and who will end up paying
the full price for his hidden arrangement."
-Alice Miller, 1997

Pain in childhood tends to induce inward focusing. As you mature, you will need to look outside of yourself, rather than living in emotional solitude. If you were abused as a child, you need to know that it was never about you. It had nothing to do with you and everything to do with your abuser. Try not to take the hurt so personally. Let them have it.

If you have been wounded in the past, your current experience of pain can be turned into wisdom, based on your experience. It can provide you with a way to tap your creativity, insight, and individual gifts, if you acknowledge its impact.

Only by putting aside your fears of childhood and through acknowledging your true emotions, needs, and desires (and expressing these), can you truly heal. If you sincerely dedicate energy toward healing, it is even possible for your pain, hurt, and loss to become gifts, which is what authenticity, is all about. You can then tap into and strengthen these gifts to be used in healing you and your children, as you learn to become increasingly resilient and prevail over your wounds. In your pain you may have secretly wished for love, gentleness, validation, and serenity, with all of them seemingly out of reach. This despair is what your gifts of hope and faith are made for, so that you can bring the pain into the light, in order to not only heal yourself, but be living authentically.

When you experience an abundance of pain in childhood you often learn to be hypersensitive, as well as hypervigilant. Learn to turn your hypervigilance into a keen sense of awareness of your surroundings, including your children's suffering. In this sense, realize that you can use your pain. Pain does not have to destroy you if you use your suffering to create compassion and strength through awareness. The sooner you accept the depth of your problems, the sooner you will be able to heal. You do not have to remain a victim to your problems and pain. Facing your pain creates freedom.

If you choose denial over honesty, then you will be more likely to be defensive or disregard or attack your child. However, doing this to someone who is smaller and weaker is only a way for you to hide yourself from your own feelings of helplessness and vulnerability. The choice is simple—do not do this. If your pain is displaced and projected onto your child (who is not responsible for harming you), then you are unjust and responsible for perpetuating further pain in your child, which only serves to perpetuate your own pain, shame, and guilt. It builds a heavily fortified wall around yourself, which eventually becomes a self-imposed prison from which you may never escape and is impenetrable by your children, as well as anyone else.

Remember

Be true to yourself!

Do not refuse to face your own history. Liberate yourself! Shine some light on that which is dark. You cannot recover a lost childhood, but you can find integrity and healing through recognition. You must fully and genuinely feel your sadness and grieve the loss of childhood so that you can move on, knowing it is in the past. As you let go of your pain you will be letting go of the inflictor(s) of that pain. This is forgiveness. It allows you to be set free from the repetitious tapes you play in your mind about the pain and anger. You are not to forgive the act, but the actor with all of his or her human weaknesses, confusions, and inability to skillfully interact with another person.

Remember

"Hatred never ceases by hatred;
But by love alone is healed…"
-Buddhist Scripture,
the Dhammapada

By forgiving others, you can see them as human, struggling through life just as you are and thus, you honor yourself in a loving way. This also teaches your children forgiveness. The need for survival comes out of vulnerability (victim and perpetrator both) and people can do some pretty destructive things to survive, often unknowingly. If you have hurt your children, making amends is restorative and alleviates guilt, shame, and remorse. So, be humble and ask for forgiveness from your children.

Reflection

"The weak can never forgive.
Forgiveness is the attribute of the strong."
-Mahatma Gandhi

Parents must be a mirror for their child, strong and accepting. Do not try to fulfill your needs through your child simply because they were not fulfilled by your parents; rather discover healing through helping your child to heal. The more you genuinely model the expression of feelings and reflect feelings back to your child, the less fragile you and your child will be. Your child's self-esteem will be strengthened and he or she will have confidence in personal feelings, wishes, desires, and needs. On the other hand, denial or rejection of feelings, high demands in spite of pain, and insensitivity, all create a loss of self in you and your child.

Prescription for helping parents heal

- ♥ Listen more carefully
- ♥ Express feelings honestly
- ♥ Face the past and deal with it
- ♥ Work on forgiveness for self and others
- ♥ Be good to yourself
- ♥ Be aware of yourself and others to intuit motivations, feelings, hopes, despair, and pain
- ♥ Do not hide in the secrets
- ♥ Journal your feelings
- ♥ Uncover the lessons in old wounds and apply them to your life
- ♥ Find support and ask for help from friends and family
- ♥ Be open to professional help and seek if necessary

Healing Wounded Families

If *you* choose to remain in hiding and ignore your child's pain, as well, you will find that your entire family will suffer. The more you practice life through a pseudo self (a false self), the more distant you get from your true self. If there has been abuse in your family, do not allow your family to be shrouded in the darkness of pain and secrets.

Keeping shameful family secrets hidden can leave your children at risk. Oftentimes, defiance, depression, or suicide is a subconscious way for a child to reveal the "family secret."

Reflection

Adolescent defiance and even suicide rates tend to increase in families unable to tolerate crisis and those which often utilize patterns of repeated yelling, hostility, and aggression.

Some families do not understand how much a child is hurting or refuse to believe the pain is real or justified. Healing is not about confrontation, blame, or revenge. When wounds within the family are first encountered and attended to, it can be scary; however, this is a fear which can be alleviated through genuine effort to face the pain. Continuing to step around it or on the other hand, pretend it does not exist, will only serve to create emotional, interactional, and spiritual emptiness and despair amongst every member of the family system.

So you do not have to hide anymore. By revealing what has been concealed, you are accepting your children and reestablishing a sense of control and security. This builds resiliency, competence, and self-assurance in all family members. Practice utilizing specific gifts such as, being available, gentle, and attentive. Cultivating your gifts of empathy, understanding, patience, faith, and healing, is of course, essential.

Family sorrow does not have to be endured. Genuinely approaching family pain can create a sense of belonging, safety, abundance, and an awakening to peace. Living in regret of bad choices will only compound problems. To renew the togetherness in your family as you heal, engage in activities such as family meetings, regular routines (e.g., bedtime, mealtime), and performing necessary rituals (e.g., cemetery visits after the loss of a loved one), as you attempt to reconnect. Live with value and purpose in individual and family health and you will find rich and rewarding paths to healing in this life and the next. You need not be perfect, only willing to persevere through love, faith, and hope.

Remember

"All healing requires gentleness,
attention, and care."
-Wayne Muller, 1992

Prescription for helping families heal

- ♥ Acknowledge the pain instead of hiding
- ♥ Share true feelings with other family members
- ♥ Share your thoughts with other family members
- ♥ Commit to working on wounds together
- ♥ Be humble
- ♥ Listen attentively
- ♥ Be honest
- ♥ Seek professional help if necessary
- ♥ Accept help when it's offered

Remember, children get hurt. Sometimes they are wounded by their parents. Sometimes it is the world that hurts them. Other times it is purely circumstantial events that lead to pain. Fortunately, there is no one in the world who is better equipped to help them heal than you are. Children are most comforted when their parents show them genuine tenderness and understanding. By following the examples above you can use your authentic gifts to help your child, your family, and yourself to heal and move on.

Questions to Consider

1. How have your children been wounded?
2. How have you been wounded in the past?
3. How has your family been wounded?
4. What can you do today that will help your child, self, and family heal?

Chapter 9

Authentic Traditions

"For where your treasure is, there also will your heart be."
-Matt. 6:21, NAS

Authentic traditions are the routines and rituals derived from the heart of a family. They are maintained as a legacy of love passed down from generation to generation which reflects who you are and what you value. Children fondly remember traditions from home and often attempt to recreate them as adults with their own families, lovingly passing on those meaningful memories.

There are a multitude of traditions stemming from various religious backgrounds, to daily ways of living, or any belief systems based on individualistic values. They may be unique to your family or they may be more universal to the society and culture you live in. From the very basic of routines surrounding meals and bedtime to momentous occasions of weddings and graduations, all provide opportunity for family bonding and add to the art of living authentically.

It is important to acknowledge these past traditions and even design some of your own. It is worth every well thought out moment, every minute spent in planning and preparation, to create something special for your family. As the adage goes, "home is where the heart is." Fortunately, you get to decide how much of your heart you will put into your home. You must know that creating memories for your children during their youngest years which reflect your authenticity builds a strong foundation that will weather the storms of adolescence.

First, you will want to consider the memories, rituals, and traditions that were the most meaningful to you as a child. Think about special times spent with your parents, grandparents, and extended family members. Keep in mind your family history, culture, and religion. Revive your family history with cooking, special occasions, language, and everyday routines. Sharing yourself, your values, and your history is the key to creating strong family connections and authentic traditions that will stand the test of time.

Remember

The best traditions come out of
meaningful connections made to heritage.

Begin with the basics. The idea in creating basic traditions is to provide routines that offer sameness, comfort, and security to your children. By basic traditions, we mean those daily and weekly comforts that form the foundation of their childhood. Bedtime and mealtime rituals can make these common problem areas more manageable with young children and more meaningful for older children. The more familiar and predictable routines become, the more they will provide a sense of stability for your children, giving them something to look forward to every day.

Bedtime Rituals

When creating your bedtime ritual, the most important thing to remember is routine, routine, routine. This is the key to smooth transitions to bedtime, especially for younger children. Establish a timeline that works for you and your children. Take your cue from their temperament as far as setting a bedtime. However, keep in mind that most children and teenagers (as well as adults) are sleep deprived. Children until the approximate age of twelve need at least ten hours of sleep per night and younger children need even more. Keep in mind, though, that when your teenager sleeps in on the weekend, rather than laziness, it can be an attempt to catch-up on what he or she lacked during the week (Yes, adolescents need of a lot of sleep).

When you begin to set up a bedtime routine for your children, start by winding them down. Limit horseplay, T.V., and sibling squabbles before bedtime. Make the household peaceful. When your children do go to bed, let them feel safe with nightlights, stuffed animals, comfortable mattresses and blankets, whatever they need, and plenty of reassurance from you. The bedtime routine is a process, not a five second command of, "Get your pajamas on, brush your teeth, and get into bed."

Be consistent. Bedtime is a time of separation for children and can be loaded with daytime anxieties. It takes time to get into a routine that works, but it is well worth it for the whole family. You may need to "shut" the entire house down at first so that your children can see that nighttime is for everyone to rest. That means you must model good sleep habits, even if you are usually a night owl. As a parent, you probably are not getting enough sleep anyway. You and your children will feel more rested and rejuvenated and get off to a better start in the morning.

Be prepared for problems. When parents change their behavior, children inevitably react. Explain the new routine to your child early in the day, and follow through. Do not give in to their whines for more time, but try to be flexible, as well. It may not work out exactly as you plan and you may need a back-up plan. Children do get sick. They do have nightmares. They have accidents. In general, children have bad days...and nights. They are human just as you are. Even after you have been consistent with your routine, things will change.

Allow for exceptions without letting go of your boundaries and limits. When problems occur, respond with tenderness and return to your routine as soon as you are able to.

After you have successfully established a bedtime routine that works for your family, you can begin to introduce special bedtime rituals. These may include a special snack before bed, singing songs while your child brushes his or her teeth, putting dolls or animals to bed, engaging in prayer, or story-time. Whatever activities you decide upon is entirely up to you and what is important to your family. Just remember not to let things get too complicated because what you establish will have to stay the same to become a tradition. If these activities become a "headache" for you, take *too* long, or start driving you "crazy," then you will not be able to establish a routine that will endure long-term. So, keep it simple, make it enjoyable, and be sensitive to your child's individuality.

Mealtime Rituals

In developing a mealtime ritual, keep it simple. Brainstorm with your family about what foods everybody likes to eat and start talking about nutrition and good food choices for the entire family. Save complicated dishes for special occasions. Make sure to keep your schedule in mind when designing your meals. Five-course homemade meals are probably not an option when you work sixty hours per week. However, you can find a way to feed your children nutritious meals at home by being creative, having your children help, and coming up with some standby meals that are easily heated and served.

The point is to make mealtime something special. It is a time to be nourished physically and emotionally. This is where manners are learned, table etiquette is established, and lives are shared.

Eat together as often as possible. This cannot be stressed enough. Families today spend very little time together. Meals provide a perfect opportunity to relax and share the day. It affords your family the chance to reconnect after work and school are done. Keep in mind your streamlining exercise from chapter 7 and make room in your schedule so that experiencing dinner with your children is a priority. It may be tempting to feed your children separately from you, but they learn that meal time is family time when you are present at the table.

Remember
Maintaining the mealtime ritual
makes it more likely that even
your teenager will show up at the dinner table.

As you consider simplifying your life, commit to making the same meal for everyone. Avoid making different things for finicky eaters. Include at least one thing that each child will like and make your children at least try the things they say they do not like. Encourage them to help choose menus for meals and assist with preparation. This activity makes them more likely to eat what is in front of them.

Do not forget that children learn good nutritional habits from their parents. So, model healthy eating habits for them, not extreme dieting or overeating. Various studies have shown that children who regularly eat nutritious meals, consistently do better in school and have better attitudes toward people and life, in general. Stock-up on nutritional snacks and make them available. The more you encourage healthy habits for your children, the more these habits are likely to last into adulthood.

Teach table manners. This is your daily opportunity to civilize your little ones. This is one of many concepts they will not learn in school. Encourage their efforts in practicing their manners. Model good table behavior, and excuse unruly children until they can rejoin the family peacefully. One thing that is often missing from today's household is an appreciation for good table manners. It is more than apparent in restaurants where unruly children are endured by patrons in amazement at a parent's lack of control. It is obvious when children are well-behaved in public restaurants that they have learned these important lessons at home.

Include your children in preparation and clean-up of meals. You are not their servants and your home is not a five-star hotel. Even young children can help set and clear the table, retrieve condiments, and wipe down placemats. Older children can help prepare meals and wash dishes. Give each of your children a place in the family.

Let them know they belong by providing them with a role in the set-up and clearing of the family table. Even if it seems like a distraction at first and you know you could accomplish these tasks much more efficiently alone, let them in. This is quality time. Your kitchen will be warmed by the presence of your little ones and they will have a cherished memory of preparing family meals with Mom and Dad.

Lastly, make mealtime pleasant. Make connections with your children during this time. Ask questions, encourage conversation, and tell them what you are grateful for. Mealtime can be something you all look forward to, instead of a battleground.

Special Occasions

There is an endless supply of reasons to celebrate, but many are yearly hallmarks to make special for your family. The following are suggestions for making holidays of any sort the kind that build memories and special bonds.

Birthdays

These can be all day events tailor made to make the birthday person feel special. One idea is to start at breakfast with "Birthday Pancakes." These are just regular pancakes, but with candles. The child gets to make a wish first thing in the morning instead of waiting until there is a cake or party. You can design your child's birthday however you wish, but consider staying simple, not elaborate, while making it special for them. Birthday parties do not have to cost a fortune. By being creative and using your gifts, you can come up with something that is in your budget, but is just perfect for that child.

Holidays

Holidays are your chance to tap into the resources of older relatives. Find out how they celebrated holidays in the past and see if you can revive some forgotten traditions from your heritage. Include your children in the preparation of holiday meals, decorating, and religious services. You may build a ginger bread house together every Christmas, or hang your flag on the Fourth of July, or always go to the Grandparents' house for Thanksgiving. Whatever these traditions are, keep them consistent and do them together.

One great idea that not only makes holidays special, but also reinforces values, is volunteering. Getting children involved in donating time to a homeless shelter, a nursing home, or giving usable items or toys to children in need, takes the focus off of what they are going to receive and places it on what they can give. Help them experience and appreciate joy in the giving of their time, their talents, and their treasures. Generosity builds integrity, empathy, and dignity. Holidays are celebrations of love for the family, the individual, and others.

Appreciation days

Similar to birthdays, events like Mothers Day, Fathers Day, Grandparents Day, or Teachers Day gives children the opportunity to plan for something special that they can do for someone else. This is about showing gratitude and you can help children learn this and to be creative while thinking of others. Encourage your children to share their special gifts and talents with the person they wish to honor. Gifts can be from the heart, like drawings or letters written to Godparents, songs for Grandparents, coupons for chores for Mom and Dad, or handmade projects for teachers. Educate your children about thoughtfulness when giving gifts and sharing appreciation.

Vacations

Plan some kind of getaway annually. If you can, let there be at least one place that you and your family visit every year, such as Grandma's house or a summer home. Consider camping trips or visits to the beach. For instance, your summer spot might be the beach, but at different locations for variety. Again, it does not have to cost a fortune, but the sameness and regularity of going back year after year to a summer getaway provides comfort and something to look forward to.

If your situation allows, take more than one vacation. This can be achieved in endless ways. Some families participate in winter activities and summer activities. Other families go somewhere one or two weekends per month. A family may take one major vacation for a month or two per year. It is up to you, but everyone needs time off and a chance to get away—children and parents—so make it happen.

Seasonal

Provide children with a role in the changing of the seasons. The beginning of school, for instance, can involve a tradition of preparation by reading together and school shopping. Winter traditions may include holiday preparation and baking. The arrival of spring can be a signal for planting a garden or the annual spring cleaning of closets, toys, outgrown clothes, or books. Summer traditions can include outdoor dinners and campouts. Think of the things you remember from your childhood that really stick out as warm memories and then try to create your own traditions that will be meaningful to your children.

Once in a Lifetime Moments

These are the momentous events that become the touch-points, and maybe even turning points, of your life. Make these traditions special by incorporating your values and gifts into your celebrations.

Coming of Age

Coming of age celebrations can be a significant occasion for the youngster and his or her entire family. In the Hispanic culture, for example, this time is marked for girls at the age of fifteen by the traditional Quinceañera, a big party and Catholic service revealing that she has become a young lady and is now old enough to date. In the Jewish culture, Bar Mitzvah and Baht Mitzvah, which take place usually at the ages of twelve and thirteen, respectively, mark the coming of age of their male and female teens. Another option to celebrate the coming of age of your child is a special dinner with parents and the designing of a "purity contract." This includes a discussion of sex and growing up and a signed contract by the child to remain pure until marriage. It may even involve the giving of a ring as a symbol of that contract. All of these are perfect opportunities to fine-tune your child's understanding of dating and responsibility, now that they are growing up.

Graduations

Commencement ceremonies are of great importance to you and your children. Think about what you would have wanted yours to be like or what it was like. The idea in creating graduation traditions is to pass on that sense of accomplishment and possibility to your children. Consider gifts that display an interest in your child's school career thus far and that symbolize where they are going in the future. Things like photo albums with their school pictures to date, scrapbooks with awards and certificates that they have earned, or letters of pride in their accomplishments, are very meaningful and will be cherished for years to come.

Weddings

These are huge events in your child's life and can be enormously stressful. The important part of this tradition for you is to try to make the day memorable by preparing something special for them. You may want to celebrate with family heritage; give them something special of yours to take with them. Make a book of wisdom (your authentic tidbits on married life) with quotes to share with the newlywed couple. Suggest family heirlooms to wear and special foods to be served that reflect your heritage. Acknowledge their preferences, while making yourself available for suggestions and guidance.

Deaths/Funerals

Commemorate the loss of a loved one with a family tradition. You may want to make a special event of bringing flowers to the grave-site or attending religious services on anniversaries of the loved one and holidays. This can help you and your children to process the pain of loss and cherish life. Help your children remember the good memories by sharing stories and treasured possessions of a loved one with them. Even if it is a pet, help them reminisce and deal with the loss, as you would any family member. These are important life events and children need to be included in the circle of life and death.

Births

The birth of a sibling, cousin, or friend's baby can be a wonderful learning experience for your child and a perfect opportunity for a new tradition to be born. Help your child think of a special gift for the new baby and its family. If it is a sibling, you can make or buy your child a t-shirt that says, "I'm a big brother/sister" and let him or her tour the hospital where the baby will be born. A child can also help decorate the new baby's room and even share in the decision process of naming the baby. Know that involvement such as this can help your child to have positive feelings about having a new addition to the family (and curbing jealousy is always a plus).

If it is a relative's baby, make arrangements for when your child can first come to visit the new baby and bring his or her gift. You can explain to children how special babies are and share stories with them or show them pictures of when they were babies. Visiting and preparing gifts for the new baby shows children the importance of these moments and are wonderful events for you to share with them.

Overall, once in a lifetime events provide the opportunity for your family to create traditions that can be passed on to the next generation. You are building history. So, take it seriously, but have fun with it.

Family Time

Family times are the traditions that make regular days special and comforting for children. There are a plethora of possibilities and this starter list is just a beginning. Spend the time to come up with some of your own. Talk to friends, relatives, and other parents and find out what they do in their homes. Forget adopting any tradition that makes you feel uncomfortable or does not feel authentic. This is about designing your life with your family, so a good fit is paramount.

Guest of Honor

Individual special days are designed to honor a different family member once a week. This activity was suggested to us by one of the participants in our parenting class, and we liked it so much that we decided to add it to our list. The "guest of honor" is an easy way to start. Once a week, one member of the family has his or her place at the table set with the special family plate. This is a plate which stands out from the rest and can be something you and your child make together or you may want to buy one.

The person who gets the plate at their place setting is the "guest of honor" for the evening. They are released from any chores at meal time as they are the "guest." Every member of the family takes turns saying something nice about that person or something about them that they are grateful for. This tradition builds family closeness, fairness, helps children learn to tolerate times when the attention is not all on them, and enforces gratitude.

Taking Turns

This is about letting one child make the decision about what the family will have for dinner one day per week. This gives each family member a say. The child may choose a certain meal to be eaten at home. Or he or she may choose to eat out or to order a pizza. There are no hard and fast rules here except whatever stipulations you place on it, such as cost. Again, this is an event that simply promotes family togetherness and helps a child know that he or she is special and an important part of the family.

Family Meetings

These are incredibly important in keeping your family on track. They are also very beneficial to fulfilling your children's needs of acceptance, control, and security. They promote family togetherness, belongingness, and egalitarian attitudes. Family meetings are structured events with an agenda that is designed by you. Things to consider including in a family meeting are discipline issues, chores (adjustments, changes, or additions), schedules, allowances, vacation ideas, and suggestions for discussion. If there is something special coming up, this would be the perfect time to discuss it. It is the perfect opportunity to air out issues, problem-solve, and extend praise.

These meetings are not optional, but mandatory for parents and children, regardless of age. They are instrumental to keeping busy families connected and produce order and teamwork into a household. At any time, children or parents can add to the agenda by putting their ideas into a suggestion box prior to the meeting. Tough issues that cannot be dealt with immediately can be tabled for further discussion at the family meetings. This is an excellent tool that will serve you well throughout your children's childhood and on into their adolescence.

Game Night

This is a great idea to encourage family togetherness, belonging, and to teach positive interaction and adherence to rules. Children and parents can take turns choosing the game for the night. This can be a weekly or monthly event that all family members can participate in. Use this tradition as an opportunity to teach children about fairness, cooperation, and how to be good winners and losers. Game night helps children to feel important and also assists them in learning important life lessons.

Date Night/Day

It is important for your child to have alone time with you. This is especially true when you have more than one child. Again, there are many possibilities. Your date does not have to cost a fortune; it only has to be individual time spent with your child. You may want to take your son or daughter out for a soda or shopping after school. Spend time at a park, go to a movie, or have a lunch date. Whether this is something that takes place once a week or once a month, make it happen. It opens communication channels and keeps you apprised of what is occurring in your child's life. Inevitably, it will prove to be priceless time spent building and maintaining a close relationship with your child.

All of these suggestions are simply starters for you to tailor to your own family. Use them as the beginnings of your own traditions, modifying them to fit into your own authentic style. Share your ideas with family and friends. Traditions, however important they may be to raising an emotionally healthy child, are unfortunately one of the first things to go when people's lives get too hectic. So, do not let these special opportunities pass you by. Take the time to make them happen.

Love Letters Notebook

Last, but certainly not least, is possibly the most important suggestion for authentic traditions. The *Love Letters Notebook* is a collection of reflections, encouragements, and sentiments from you to your child. Your love letters are written in journal entry form and kept in a bound notebook. You can use any type of book, but the nicer the better. You can even decorate the book with stickers, drawings, or pictures that are special for each of your children.

These love letters are written strictly by the parent and are one-sided. The child has no reciprocal obligation to write back. Once the letter has been read, the *Love Letters Notebook* is returned to the parent for the next entry. Sample entries may include, "Ten things I love about you;" "Three things I am sorry for;" "I am so proud of you because..." We have provided you with additional example entries in Appendix B. This is an opportunity to share with your children the things that may be hard to say or easily forgotten.

Entries can be added to the book at any time and for any reason. It is something that you will create during your child's entire childhood. However, it is never too late to begin compiling your *Love Letters Notebook*. Even if your child is an adolescent, think about how he or she would be affected by getting a love note from you.

You can create a tradition of including the *Love Letters Notebook* and a new entry with their holiday gifts, their birthday pancakes, or on the last day of school. Memories of their babyhood, memories from your own childhood, and words of encouragement can be put on paper in a form that becomes a lifelong treasure for your child. The finished notebook can be given as a gift at a milestone event, like the day they get married or leave for college. This can be one of the most meaningful souvenirs of their childhood that you can give to your child. Take the time to indulge your children in this gift of yourself and give them the privilege of knowing how you treasure them, as well as what a gift they are to you.

Remember
Regardless of the means,
you are the beginning
of your children's legacy.

Traditions become authentic when they are a reflection of who you are as an individual and as a family. They take a lot of planning, preparation, and commitment, but the payoff is having children who feel loved, important, and have a sense of belonging to something bigger than themselves. Take the time. Do the work. It will payoff in innumerable ways for your family. Put your heart into it and create something special. Design the life you want for yourself and your children. They are worth it and so are you.

Questions to Consider

1. What traditions from your childhood were especially meaningful?
2. How can you revive your family's heritage?
3. What traditions can you implement immediately that will bring life to your authenticity?
4. How would you have felt receiving a *Love Letters Notebook* from your parents?

Chapter 10

Generating Hope

"If one advances confidently in the direction of his dreams, and endeavors to live a life which he has imagined, he will meet with a success unexpected in common hours."
-Henry David Thoreau

There is nothing righteous or just in keeping your true self from your children. Rather than peace and contentment, it makes manifest only lies, avarice, and cruelty. It is absolutely essential as a parent—and in life itself—that you demand authenticity from yourself. Do not deny a relationship with yourself or you will also deny courage, love, and laughter, as well. You will lose all relationship with others and be accompanied instead by despair and guilt. This is not what you want to teach your children.

Authenticity arises from having spent the time as an adult breaking down defense mechanisms you learned in childhood. These defense mechanisms were created out of not having your own emotional needs met and subsequently block you from having an authentic relationship with yourself and others. They begin as a very adaptive survival or coping skill; something necessary to protect you from whatever emotional or physical wounds or traumas you endured as a child. However, once you grow into adult life, it is easy to fall back into old defensive paradigms when you are feeling threatened, stressed, or criticized, rather than developing healthier ways of protecting your integrity.

Unlearning these ingrained patterns of behavior can be a major challenge, requiring you to be completely honest with yourself. Once you unlearn these patterns and put healthy ones in their place you will discover that the rewards are immense, such as increased self-esteem, self-confidence, and enhanced serenity. Until you build this true and genuine relationship with yourself, you will not have good relationships with your friends, spouse, or ultimately, your children.

The gifts we discussed in chapter 1 are the foundations of this authenticity. The more you recognize and practice them, the more authentic you will become. These gifts are natural talents and abilities that you were born with. In order to develop these gifts into strengths and be able to use them to improve the quality of your parenting, it is important to first recognize them in yourself. Then you must identify which ones you currently use efficiently and notice the obstacles which hold you back.

Know that the best gift you can give to your children is *you.* Your emotional health is contingent on getting honest, so make sure you are being truthful with yourself. Hopefully, you took the time to answer the "Questions to Consider" throughout the book and were able to discuss them with others. If not, we encourage you to go back and do so. The more you discover about yourself, your family, your children, and your parenting, the more authentic and successful you will be.

Reflection

"The moral law tells us the tune we have to play;
our instincts are merely the keys."
-C.S. Lewis, *Mere Christianity*

Having addressed the issue of gifts, strengths, and defenses propels you into a deeper understanding of what you may have missed out on as a child. This understanding provides you with the opportunity to grow toward emotional health as an adult. Chapter 2 hopefully opened your eyes to what your children may be missing out on. Fulfilling these needs for your children depends largely on how well you have managed to fulfill them for yourself as an adult, especially if they were lacking in childhood. Make sure you fully understand the magnitude of the ramifications of fulfilling vs. not fulfilling these needs for your children.

It is not too late to do this for your children. Make the effort to get to the bottom of difficult situations you are having with them. Utilize your gifts of empathy, listening, and compassion to understand where they are coming from, what is occurring beneath the surface that they may not be telling you, and what need they are misguidedly trying to fulfill through their behavior. Based on your history, consider why some of these needs may be harder than others for you to fulfill. Then deal with it. Their childhood does not have to resemble yours (unless you want it to). You are the adult now, and you can make your own choices to make a difference in your life as well as theirs.

Remember

Defenses standing in the way
of your authenticity, stem from
not having your emotional needs met
in childhood.

Understanding and maintaining a healthy, balanced family structure, is crucial to your authentic parenting. If the dynamics of your family have been through any kind of upheaval due to divorce, death of a loved one, job change, or other change or trauma, you are in need of restructuring. Children are too often the wind on which the parent's wings rest and it should be the other way around. Your children may be your inspiration, but consider their manifest potential, if instead, you are theirs.

Consequently, if you remember from chapter 3, the balance of power and authority needs to flow in a downward motion, beginning with the strength of the parents (whether single or married). The security of the children and the stability of the family depend on the united front and authority of the executive subsystem (the parents). That is, in a divorce situation, it is important to watch out for system failure when a child is brought up to peer level with the parents. This seldom achieves great results. It merely causes problems for the parents, the children, and even sibling relationships. Reconstruct your family so that the balance of power stabilizes. Do not lean on your older children. Find outside support in other adult relationships or therapy to help you through the difficult times. In order to feel secure, your children need to know that you are in charge.

Open and sincere communication is at the heart of every well-functioning relationship. All behavior is communication. Master a sense of calm and patience. Some of our most intense defense mechanisms manifest themselves in how we communicate with others. When we are under stress or feel threatened or criticized, these defensive communication styles are what will surface if left unchecked.

Reflection

"What you do speaks so loud that I cannot hear what you say."
-Ralph Waldo Emerson

Keeping your communication authentic requires you to think before speaking. With children, who are skilled professionals at pushing your buttons, it requires even more effort to keep from falling into old patterns of sarcasm, screaming, or silence. Ignoring these patterns will not make them go away, either. Paying attention to triggers, stopping to think first, and taking a relaxing breath (or two or six), will make an enormous difference in refraining from reacting with defensive patterns. The result of using careful words, an even tone, and a controlled volume is building a better relationship with your children, your family, and your friends. This is especially true when applying consequences to your children's behavior.

Discipline designed to teach is the foundation of raising healthy, well-functioning children. Using your gifts, offering suitable choices, and knowing when to dig in your heels and when to let go, are instrumental in guiding your children through the stages of childhood. You are their benchmark. They will attempt to emulate the behavior you model in your home, in public, and in your relationships.

Your commitment to improving your own values, lifestyle, and relationships directly impacts how well you will raise your children. The "Do as I say, not as I do" cliché does not hold water in child-rearing. The most important discipline technique you can start using immediately is to live a life that you and your children can be proud of. Model an authentic life, those traits and qualities that you want your children to possess, and they will follow suit.

The objective needs to be self-discipline. Take the time to figure out the consequences that make the most sense to your child's patterns of misbehavior. Teach your children manners, kindness, respect for authority, and compassion for others, at home. The world will not do this for you. Education always begins at home with unconditional love, attention, and devotion. The more you share of your true self, the more they will be able to learn from your experiences—both successes and failures.

The manner in which you handle communication and discipline issues depends in large part on how the rest of your life is managed. If you are always in a hurry, rushing from one obligation to the next and your life is becoming a mess, then your defenses are sure to rise up and affect the manner in which you handle life with your children. It is next to impossible to be authentic when you are constantly stressed, burned-out, or rushed.

Serenity cannot coexist with chaos. You will have to make some difficult, but well thought out choices. You must decide whether the benefits of running around "crazy" outweigh the costs on your physical and emotional health, your family, and your children.

Ninety-nine point nine percent of the time, they will not. It is not worth the toll it takes on your sanity to work three jobs, drive all day or over schedule yourself and your children.

Create clear boundaries around yourself and your family. Learn how to say, "No," to taxing, but meaningless activities. Insulate your family without becoming rigid and do not forget to breathe. Take the time to simply hang out with your children without having an agenda. For instance, stay in your pajamas all day and drink hot cocoa with them. Enjoy their childhood. Let them just play, pretend, experiment, daydream, and be children.

Beyond this, create structure for safety, routines for learning, and build your family traditions. Traditions are the life blood of the family. They are passed on from one generation to the next and provide the foundation for emotional and spiritual growth. They include basic rituals, times of celebration and mourning, and attention to special occasions. They are life memories in their purest form.

Do not procrastinate and let these opportunities pass you by. Prepare, plan, and include your children in the process of reviving old traditions and creating new ones. Traditions are what cherished memories are made of. You can make every day special and important days memorable, just by adding a few of your authentic touches.

Marinate your children in authentic love and provide them with memories that will last a lifetime. It is absolutely worth it to hear them say, "Mom and Dad, remember when we…" Life is a series of moments all strung together. It is up to you to decide whether they will be merely endured or absolutely cherished.

Having read this book, you have been provided with the opportunity to get real with yourself about the residual patterns of behavior from your childhood, which may have been holding you back from being the parent you always wanted to be. Awareness of old wounds, of your defenses, and your conscious attempts to deal with problem situations in a more mature and healthy way, has developed your gifts and turned them into strengths. You now know those defensive behaviors like sarcasm, passive and active aggression, over-achievement, or people-pleasing can be kept under control. Simply knowing that they exist and working on changing your behavior are the first steps toward authenticity. Your gifts are allowed to shine through when defenses are worked out.

Reflection

"If it were not for hope, the heart would break."
-Thomas Fuller

Recognizing what you do not have and aiming diligently for what you truly desire, remembering always virtue, love, and sincerity in your search, you will fulfill all of your dreams of being an exceptional parent. These hopes will provide you with the heart to endure all of life's challenges when you believe in something greater than yourself, in yourself, in your children, and the gifts that God blessed you with.

The greatest gift you can give your child is the gift of your true self. The real you is your *authentic self.* So peel the layers of defense that life and circumstance have helped you build. You no longer need them. You are a strong, capable person with children who need you. You already know there are better ways of handling difficult situations. Be brave, take the leap, go deep, and uncover the exceptional parent you were always meant to be.

Appendix A

Development

It has long been known that we all develop through stages, although some believe the stages to be more fluid, while others believe them to have specific starting and stopping points. There are also different types of development, including social, cognitive, emotional, physiological, and moral. In the following pages, we will discuss the different stages in each type of development, including general tasks that children attempt to achieve at each stage.

The importance of helping you to understand children's developmental stages is to give parents knowledge of what to expect from their children, so that they can gauge appropriate interaction skills and minimize frustration through this awareness. The more clearly parents comprehend these developmental stages, the more likely they will be able to assist their children in smooth transitions.

Maslow's Hierarchy of Motivational Needs

Every human being is born with a motivation toward forward growth and possesses certain needs that must be fulfilled before this growth can take place. We have already discussed the main three intrinsic emotional needs, acceptance, control, and security, but we must not forget the physical needs which are a prerequisite to psychological growth and emotional health.

Abraham Maslow is most famous for teaching us that every individual possesses a drive toward self-actualization (i.e., being fully functional, acting purely of one's own volition, and being satisfied and content). He purported that the physical needs of each person must be met first, however, in order for the individual to move forward in an attempt to reach emotional and spiritual fulfillment. Maslow's hierarchy depicts his concept of motivational needs (see fig. 3).

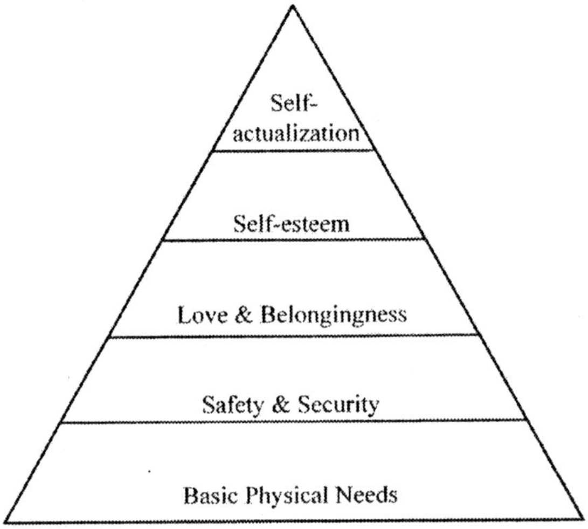

Figure 3. Maslow's hierarchy of motivational needs. Basic needs must be met before proceeding to higher needs, however individuals fluctuate between these higher needs at different times in their life.

Maslow's hierarchy of motivational needs

If an individual is missing the essential human needs at the bottom of the pyramid, then it is unreasonable to expect a person to have the capability to move up. Everybody needs a foundation from which to work. Maslow insisted that meeting a person's basic needs (i.e. air, food, water, shelter, and clothing) is a prerequisite of moving toward the top of the hierarchy in this paradigm. The four stages that lie above "Basic Physical Needs" on the hierarchy are more flexible, with people moving in and out of them throughout their lives, as they continually strive for self-actualization.

That being said, it is of some significance to acknowledge that although behavioral techniques to child rearing have become a mainstay of Western societies, the fulfillment of inner needs of children mixed with behavioral interventions at a young age, will cultivate a healthier adolescent and thus, young adult. By assuring children's emotional needs are met, most of the behavioral components of discipline can eventually be adopted by the adolescent and incorporated into their own self-monitoring mechanism.

Young children do not have the insight or logical thinking necessary for adequate decision-making. But as adolescents become more reality-based and begin to think abstractly, they are able to make decisions autonomously without their parents being the general managers of their lives.

Therefore, it is your job as a parent, to make sure that your children are given the tools necessary to move up this hierarchy. Hopefully, each person can ultimately reach a point of better understanding of human components such as truth, goodness, beauty, transcendence, uniqueness, unity, justice, order, and simplicity. These are the values that individuals can emulate when they are at their best.

Psychosocial Development

The psychosocial model of human development is derived from Erik Erikson (1902-1994) who views children as developing through psychosocial crises during stages which are expressed as polarities (e.g., Trust vs. Mistrust). Individuals must experience the contrasting conditions of each developmental turning point through normal experiences of frustration and disappointment in their attempt to resolve each crisis. How individuals resolve these crises shapes how they view life, their level of motivation and determination, and their commitment to living a valuable existence.

Individuals then are developing and changing throughout their entire lifespan, according to Erikson, as they confront these unique developmental crises at each stage. Although we only include stages passing through adolescence, you can see in table 7, that each crisis a person faces is an opportunity for enhanced aptitude and capability (adaptive resolution) or uncertain ineptness (maladaptive resolution).

Table Erikson's psychosocial development

Life stage	Psychosocial crisis
Infancy (birth to approximately 1 1/2 years)	**Trust vs. Mistrust**—Infants either learn comfort and security or anxiety and ineffectiveness in the absence of their parents. This establishes the groundwork for mutuality (interdependence) and the capacity for giving to others.
Toddlerhood (approximately 1 1/2-3 years)	**Autonomy vs. Shame and Doubt**—Child learns to risk breaking the trustful relationship with the parent in order to progress in performing his or her own actions or discover that independence leads to failure and punishment.
Early school age (4-6 years)	**Initiative vs. Guilt**—Children acquire parental approval for accomplishments and a sense of responsibility, or that they are not worthy of pursuing their wishes and develop feelings of guilt.
Middle childhood (6-12 years)	**Industry vs. Inferiority**—Children are curious and have a wish to learn and either feel recognition by acquiring skills and producing things or gain a sense of failure, inadequacy, and incompetence.
Early adolescence (12-18 years)	**Identity vs. Role confusion**—Teens either establish appropriate personal, social, and sexual roles and strive toward a future occupation, or become vulnerable to others' ideologies to gain social acceptance and may fall prey to inner fragmentation.
Later adolescence (18-24 years)	**Intimacy vs. Isolation**—Young adults use their acquired sense of identity to pursue close relationships with others, or become self-absorbed, achieving no intimacy, thus having a fragile identity and losing an essential aspect of themselves.

Note: Numbers in parentheses are approximate age distribution. A stage may begin earlier or later than the first age listed and end earlier or extend beyond the second age listed for each stage.

Erikson's psychosocial development

Developmental Tasks Associated with Children's Stages

In table 8 you can see the general tasks which children attempt to achieve during each stage in their development. Some children successfully complete these tasks at earlier or later ages than others; therefore these are average estimates of completion for each life stage.

Table Developmental task achievment

Life Stage	Developmental Tasks
Infancy (births to 2 years)	Sensory, perceptual, and motor functions Attachment and bonding Social connectedness Understanding the nature and classification of objects Early emotional development
Toddlerhood (2-3 years)	Mastering locomotion and motor skills Increased imagination Development of language skills Self-regulation and impulse control
Early school age (4-6 years)	Gender role identification Values acquired from parents Perspective taking Self-awareness and differentiation Interaction with peers Basic skills of education
Middle childhood (6-12 years)	Social development and friendship Skill learning and competence Self-efficacy Introspection and self-evaluation Value of team play and cooperation
Early adolescence (12-18 years)	Puberty and physical maturation Variability in emotional development Affiliation with the peer group, rather than parents Abstract thinking Sexual relationships
Later adolescence (18-24 years)	Personal identity and role experimentation Autonomy from parents Meaning in emotional development Internalized morality and fidelity Career choice

Note: Numbers in parentheses are approximate age distribution. A stage may begin earlier or later than the first age listed and end earlier or extend beyond the second age listed for each stage.
Source: Adapted from Newman & Newman, 1999

Developmental task achievement

Cognitive Development

Like Erikson, Jean Piaget (1896-1980) focused on various developmental stages for humans; however he concentrated his theories specifically on cognitive development and theorized only the series of stages that an individual passes through between infancy to adolescence, rather than throughout the lifespan. These stages are qualitatively different (see table 9). That is, an individual must pass through each stage before proceeding into the next. As children cognitively develop, they reason very differently from one stage to the next. Many theorists have since, challenged his theories and parents must take into consideration, individual differences, culture, and a child's abilities to accommodate adequate environmental information to move through each stage. As you can see in table 8, Piaget's theory encompasses four stages: sensorimotor, preoperational, concrete operational and formal operational.

Table Piaget's stages of cognitive development

Life stage	Cognitive tasks
Sensorimotor (birth-about 2 years)	Progressively, infants learn how to organize and coordinate physical movement, sensations, and perceptions as they interact with the environment. By the end of this stage they achieve "object permanence" which is the ability to know that objects (e.g., a parent) continue to exist even when they are not in their immediate presence.
Preoperational (about 2-7 years)	At the beginning of this stage, children's egocentrism gains strength, but eventually lessens. They obtain magical thinking and begin to form concepts and mental reasoning. They use symbolic thought and creative play, becoming curious and intuitive without yet utilizing rational thinking. By the end of this stage they learn to focus their attention, as well as the conservation (permanence) of an object's attributes.
Concrete Operational (about 7-11 years)	During this stage children move from physical actions to mental ones. They learn that concrete objects can change form. Logical reasoning begins to develop and they learn to classify and divide objects, as well as comprehend interrelationships.
Formal Operational (about 11-15 years)	During this stage children move from concrete to abstract thought. They think about what and why they are thinking. As they progress through abstract, idealistic, and logical thinking, they develop hypothetical-deductive reasoning abilities through which they learn to problem-solve.

Note: Numbers in parentheses are approximate age distribution. A stage may begin earlier or later than the first age listed and end earlier or extend beyond the second age listed for each stage.

Piaget's stages of cognitive development

Moral Development

There have been multiple theories about a child's moral development put forth in the literature; however, we focus here on the theory of Lawrence Kohlberg (1927-1987), for ease of understanding. Kohlberg studied under and was influenced by Piaget and professed a cognitive perspective on an individual's moral reasoning. He contended that individuals mature morally in a fixed sequence with one stage building upon another. His theory centers on the *internalization of ideals* for behavior. Kohlberg concluded that there are three levels of development, each consisting of two stages. It is interesting to note that studies have shown that perhaps only 10% of the general population ever reaches stage 5 and that it is extremely rare for individuals to reach stage 6.

Level One (before the age of 9)—Preconventional Reasoning

Stage 1: Obedience and punishment orientation—Children obey because they are told to obey and to avoid punishment. Morality is external.

Stage 2: Individualism and purpose—Children obey because it is in their best interest and they may be rewarded. There is no identification with external values.

Level Two (early to late adolescence)—Conventional Reasoning

Stage 3: Interpersonal norms—Children want to be seen as "good" and therefore, adopt the moral standards of their parents. They learn to value trust, loyalty, and caring in this stage. They function with good motives.

Stage 4: Maintenance of social order—Children make moral judgments based on society's standards of order, law, justice, and duty.

Level Three (over 20 years old if achieved)—Postconventional Reasoning

Stage 5: Social contract vs. individual rights—Individuals understand that values are more important than law and therefore, laws are relative. They consider the rights, values, meaning, and purpose within society.

Stage 6: Universal principles—Individuals solve conflict by making decisions which rest on internalized moral standards based on universal human rights, such as dignity and respect for all. They follow conscience rather than law, which may involve civil disobedience, even at risk to themselves.

Moral development begins with you. How you live your life and the lifestyle modeled for your children is the foundation of their moral development. Encourage their understanding of right and wrong. Ask them open-ended questions and find out where they are at in their development. Analyze and evaluate with them what they are exposed to in the media. Address those moral issues that are in the news and find out what they think. Have necessary discussions so that they will know exactly where you stand. Live a moral life and make good choices they can see and model. Even the little things count because your children are always watching you for their example.

Child Abuse

We include this section in order to educate parents as to how the law visualizes child abuse and to assist parents in raising their awareness of their own behaviors. Hopefully, this can arouse the potential willingness to seek help if parents are experiencing any of these difficulties.

Child abuse has existed throughout history, but here in the United States, the Federal Child Abuse Prevention and Treatment Act was not enacted until 1974. Obviously, it took awhile to take this seriously. The definition of child abuse has also changed over the years, as moral values, social expectations, and treatment services have evolved. Indeed, reported incidents of child abuse have steadily increased over the last thirty years, although it is uncertain as to whether this is due to the increased resources, increased incidence, reduced tolerance, or increased acknowledgment (rather than family secret-keeping) of society.

What Is Child Abuse?

Physical abuse

Physical abuse is any intentional (i.e., non-accidental) act that results in physical injury. Parents who inflict direct injury on their children do so with deliberate assaults, such as punching, slapping, throwing, burning, biting, hair-pulling, cutting, poking, twisting limbs, or any kind of torture. Physical injury of children most often represents unjustifiable or unreasonably severe corporal punishment—not reasonable corporal punishment—and is considered *child abuse* when injuries are inconsistent with explanations or history, are unexplained, or leave marks (e.g., welts, bleeding, etc.) on the child.

A child can also be considered to be in danger (thus a reportable situation) when there is threatened harm that could actually result in serious injury to him or her and the parent is seen as capable of such behavior because of conditions like mental illness or past abuse. Even a parent's failure to protect a child from another's maltreatment, is seen as abusive. In any event, although spanking a child on the bottom with your hand is not considered child abuse, we do not justify the necessity of this behavior if discipline designed to teach is consistently and judiciously applied.

Physical neglect

Although many children are severely injured or die each year from unreasonable physical abuse, more children than you may think, die from neglect. This is the epitome of not meeting your child's basic needs, as Maslow would contend. Neglect is the negligent treatment or maltreatment of the child in which a parent fails to provide adequate care. It indicates harm or threatened harm to the child's health or welfare, including physical, emotional, or social deprivation.

General neglect is the negligent failure of a parent or caretaker to provide adequate nutrition, clothing, shelter, hygiene, medical care, or supervision where no physical injury to the child has occurred (Besharov, 1990; County, 2004). This includes leaving young children without adequate supervision. **Severe neglect** is the negligent failure of a parent or caretaker to protect the child from severe malnutrition or medically diagnosed non-organic failure to thrive. This means that parents willfully cause or permit the child (or health of the child) to be in danger.

Emotional abuse

Emotional abuse is any non-physical act that can handicap a child emotionally or intellectually (County, 2004). This includes verbal assaults such as belittling, screaming, threatening, blaming, sarcasm, shaming, or humiliating your child. Unpredictable responses which often come from excessively distorted parental attitudes and actions, continual negative moods, constant family discord, and double-bind messages in your communication can also be emotionally abusive. When a parent does not provide adequate and normal life experiences which produce feelings of want, need, security, worth, or love to a child, it falls in the category of emotional deprivation, as we have already discussed.

Sexual abuse

Sexual abuse can be inflicted in many different forms. It is defined as sexual assault of a minor and includes contact, penetration, exploitation, or exhibitionism.

Sexual **assault** includes rape (or allowing such rape), incest, sodomy, oral copulation, penetration of genital or anal openings by a foreign object, and child molestation (just a single incident). Sexual **exploitation** is engaging a minor in obscene acts or coercion of a child to engage in prostitution. This includes depicting a child in or creating, developing, or trading photos of children engaged in obscene sexual conduct. **Exhibitionism** means that an adult cannot expose themselves to a child or ask a child to expose himself or herself to the adult with the intent of coercion. In addition, they must not do these things with the purpose of sexual gratification, arousal, or degradation.

Sometimes the maltreatment of children is unintended or due to ignorance, although this is no excuse in the eyes of the law. When parents are stressed, tired, frustrated, or overwhelmed, they may inexplicably lash-out verbally or physically toward their children. Often, parents have been abused themselves or have experienced deprived childhoods, subsequently creating the same destructive environment for their children that their parents provided for them. They may even reverse roles with their children, expecting and demanding love and care from their offspring while having difficulty returning these emotional necessities to their children. Parents may also simply lack understanding of children's basic needs and capabilities.

Parents must learn to remove themselves from highly charged situations if need be, to be patient with their children's behaviors, and most important, to pay attention to their own emotions which may be welling-up beneath the surface. Parents can walk away, essentially taking their own time-out, do some deep breathing exercises, and cool themselves down before deciding on how to handle a highly charged situation.

By being self-aware, parents can learn to control their emotional reactions before mishaps occur with their children, paving the way for finding positive solutions to the problem. If parents are not capable of gaining this control, they should seek available assistance, so that they and their children can enjoy happy, healthy lives together.

Domestic Violence

Domestic violence between adults can be extremely damaging to children. Although parents may think that this behavior is between themselves and their significant other, children are inevitable emotionally disturbed by overt or covert acts of domestic violence. This is why it is so important for you to examine your life and yourself as a parent, so that you may become aware of your actions. Where did you learn to be a victim and/or perpetrator of this behavior?

Consider the fact also, that domestic violence commonly occurs, and increases in frequency and intensity, in homes where there is alcohol or drug use. Domestic violence is considered child abuse when it presents a danger to children that are present in the home. When it places a child in the position of potential physical danger or results in mental suffering (which is "willful cruelty"), then it is considered abusive (County, 2004).

Internet Exploitation

Keep in mind, that the internet provides a virtual playground of cyberspace for child sexual predators. They have the opportunity to engage children in anonymous exchanges that often lead to personal questions designed to assess whether the child can be lured into sexual conversation and sexual contact. It has also become a venue of choice for predators that transmit and receive child pornography.

As parents, your job is to help children understand why they should not give out personal information (including their e-mail), no matter how friendly someone may be on a website or in a chat room. Let them know that they can come to you if they are receiving messages that make them feel uncomfortable, so that you can read them for yourself. Set-up guidelines that deal specifically with meeting people on the internet, and keep the computer in a high traffic part of the house, such as the living room, so that you may easily monitor your children's activities without making them feel as if you are watching over their shoulders at all times. We have provided resources for you which may be helpful:

Resources for Your Family

Childhelp USA® National Child Abuse Hotline
http://www.childhelpusa.org
1-800-4A-CHILD

National Council on Child Abuse and Family Violence
http://www.nccafv.org
1025 Connecticut Avenue NW
Washington, DC 20036
(202) 429-6695

National Runaway Switchboard
http://www.nrscrisisline.org
1-800-RUNAWAY

Runaway Hotline
1-800-448-4630

National Council on Alcohol and Drugs
1-800-475-HOPE

Drug Abuse Hotline and Information
1-800-662-HELP

The National Alcohol and Substance Abuse Information Call Center
http://addictioncareoptions.com
1-800-784-6776

The National Women's Health Information Center
U.S. Department of Health and Human Services
Office on Women's Health
http://www.4woman.gov/violence/state.cfm
1-800-994-WOMAN

National Domestic Violence Hotline
1-800-799-SAFE

Rape, Abuse, & Incest National Network
http://www.rainn.org

National Sexual Assault Hotline
1-800-656-4673

National Center for Posttraumatic Stress Disorder
http://www.ncptsd.org
(802)296-6300

You can find a clearinghouse of resources at:
http://www.healthyplace.com/site/resources.htm

Supplemental Reading Bibliography

We list here some of the resources that have helped to form many of our ideas in our practice and in the making of this book, although not directly utilized within the text. This is not an exhaustive list and there are a multitude of other books that could be helpful to the reader. These are works which we believe may expressly assist you in becoming the authentic parent you always wanted to be.

Borba, M. (1999). *Parents Do Make a Difference: How to Raise Kids with Solid Character, Strong Minds, and Caring Hearts.* Indianapolis, IN: Jossey-Bass.

Brooks, R. & Goldstein, S. (2001). *Raising Resilient Children: Fostering Strength, Hope, and Optimism in Your Child.* New York: Contemporary Books.

Collins, M. (1996). *Values: Lighting the Candle of Excellence: A Practical Guide for the Family.* Los Angeles, CA: Dove Books.

Faber, A. & Mazlish, E. (1999). *How to Talk So Kids Will Listen and Listen So Kids Will Talk.* New York: Harper Collins.

Fortune, D. & Fortune, K. (1989). *Discover Your Children's Gifts.* Grand Rapids, MI: Chosen Books.

Glasser, H. & Easley, J. (1998). *Transforming the Difficult Child: The Nurtured Heart Approach.* Nashville, TN: Vaughan Printing.

Gordon, T. (1975). *Parent Effectiveness Training: The Tested New Way to Raise Responsible Children.* New York: Plume.

Greenspan, S. & Salmon, J. (1996). *The Challenging Child: Understanding, Raising, and Enjoying the Five "Difficult" Types of Children.* Cambridge, MA: Perseus Books.

Greydanus, D. E. & Bashe, P. (Eds.). (2003). *Caring For Your Teenager.* New York: Bantam Books.

Kindlon, D. & Thompson, M. (2000). *Raising Cain: Protecting the Emotional Life of Boys.* New York: Ballantine Books.

McGraw, P. C. (2001). *Self Matters: Creating Your Life from the Inside Out.* New York: Free Press.

McGraw, P. C. (2004). *Family First: Your Step-by-Step Plan for Creating a Phenomenal Family.* New York: Free Press.

Nelson, J. (1996). *Positive Discipline: The Classic Guide for Parents and Teachers to Help Children Develop Self-discipline, Responsibility, Cooperation, and Problem-solving skills.* New York: Ballantine Books.

Newmark, G. (1999). *How to Raise Emotionally Healthy Children: Meeting the Five Critical Needs of Children…and Parents too!* Tarzana, CA: NMI Publishers.

Nolte, D. L. (1998). *Children Learn What they Live: Parenting to Inspire Values.* New York: Workman Publishing.

Philadelphia Child Guidance Center (1994). *Your Child's Emotional Health: The Essential Guide to Every Facet of a Child's Psychological and Mental Development, from Age Six to Age Thirteen.* New York: Macmillan.

Pipher, M. (1994). *Reviving Ophelia: Saving the Selves of Adolescent Girls.* New York: Ballantine Books.

Riera, M. (2003). *Staying Connected To Your Teenager: How to Keep Them Talking to You and How to Hear What They're Really Saying.* Cambridge, MA: Perseus Publishing.

Rocks, C. (2001). *Organizing the Good Life: A Joyful Path to Joyful Simplicity—Home to Work and Back.* Tempe, AZ: Facts On Demand Press.

St. James, E. (2000). *Simplify Your Life with Kids: 100 Ways to Make Family Life Easier and More Fun.* Kansa City, MO: Andrews McMeel Publishing.

Thomas, K. (1999). *Simplicity: Finding Peace by Uncluttering Your Life.* Nashville, TN: Broadman and Holman Publishers.

Turansky, S. & Miller, J. (2002). *Good and Angry: Exchanging Frustration for Character…In You and Your kids.* Colorado Springs, CO: Waterbrook Press.

Appendix B

Quality Time

What does quality time actually mean? It means sharing life with your children. It is not some enigma that explicitly differs from quantity time. Any time that you spend talking to your children, interacting on a genuine and attentive level can be seen as quality time, and the quantity of quality time you expend is crucial to the healthy development of your children. We have provided you with a list of some common opportunities for you to engage in quality time with your children:

♥ Making a meal—your child can set the table or help you prepare the meal.
♥ Putting your child to bed—read a story or have them read to you, or talk about specific concerns.
♥ Eating dinner together as a family and discussing the day's events
♥ Playing board games as a family
♥ Watching movies/videos as a family—don't forget to let your child choose sometimes
♥ Discussing things your children watch on T.V. or in movies
♥ Participating in your child's homework process
♥ Taking time to go outdoors, such as to the park, a sports engagement, or camping
♥ Discussing their concerns—for instance, friends or school
♥ Going out to dinner as a family

The point is, take the time to enjoy your children. Find things that they enjoy and continually try to make them a part of the process. Focus on your child rather than the activity itself and how you are interacting with your child. Remember, it is not all about you. It *is* all about them.

More specific ideas for spending quality time with your child

- ♥ Notice how the moon changes each night
- ♥ Draw a picture together
- ♥ Find your city on a map
- ♥ Go to a museum
- ♥ Listen to music together
- ♥ Take pictures of your family
- ♥ Take a walk
- ♥ Gather old toys to give to a charity
- ♥ Make a family tree
- ♥ Collect leaves & other elements of nature
- ♥ Go to the library
- ♥ Have a picnic in the backyard or at a park
- ♥ Read together
- ♥ Sing songs together
- ♥ Decorate a shoebox to store treasures in
- ♥ Take your child out to lunch
- ♥ Make a beaded necklace
- ♥ Daydream together
- ♥ Look at family photo album
- ♥ Write a story or poem together
- ♥ Bake treats together
- ♥ Plant flowers outdoors
- ♥ Send a postcard to a friend
- ♥ Explore with a flashlight
- ♥ Do an art project together
- ♥ Discover forms in the clouds together

Synopsis of Ideas for Fulfilling Your Child's Intrinsic Needs

♥ Look for opportunities to give positive attention to your children for achievements, for trying hard regardless of achievement, honesty, picking up after themselves, using kind words, sitting quietly, and any other positive qualities. Remember, be specific.
♥ Attend to emotional needs consistently. Encourage the expression of all feelings. Keep in mind that many parents have problems dealing with their child's anger, fear, or sadness. Acknowledging *all* feelings and attending to your children's emotional needs, lets them know that they are valued.
♥ Take the time to learn what the sources of their feelings are.
♥ Always extend respect to them.
♥ Maintain open communication channels.
♥ Utilize active listening.
♥ Let them know that you approve of them and are proud of them regardless of their accomplishments.
♥ Reinforce sincere effort.
♥ Be realistic with your expectations, dependent on your child's developmental age and capabilities, always building on strengths, while helping them expand their limitations.
♥ Praise small successes. Let your child know that you believe in him or her, nurturing an attitude of *I can do it*. If you do not believe in your child, you can be sure your child will not believe in him or herself.
♥ Provide routine, structure, and limits, modeling and teaching clear boundaries. Nurture reliable, responsible, and genuine attitudes and behavior.
♥ Keep discipline as a learning experience with consistent consequences.
♥ Provide your children opportunities to use their innate talents and encourage their participation in various activities. Accept limitations while helping them to improve.
♥ Remain positive and realistic, while modeling self-confidence, self-care, and stress healthy coping behaviors.
♥ Model honesty and genuineness.
♥ Use only positive messages to and about your children, reframing

negative labels (e.g., "observant" vs. "timid").

- ♥ Encourage uniqueness and do not compare them to their siblings or friends.
- ♥ Use discipline that is designed to teach and is fair and consistent.
- ♥ Stand firm and be clear on your values, consistently modeling them for your children.
- ♥ Be patient.

Example Entries for the *Love Letters Notebook*

- ♥ Ten things I love about you
- ♥ Three things I'm sorry for
- ♥ My wishes for you
- ♥ My favorite childhood memory (parent's)
- ♥ I'm so proud of you because…
- ♥ The cutest thing you did as a baby was…
- ♥ My thoughts the day you were born
- ♥ Something I learned the hard way
- ♥ You're terrific at…
- ♥ My hopes for you
- ♥ I feel your pain when…
- ♥ If I could turn back time to _____…
- ♥ My favorite thing to do with you is _____ because…
- ♥ You remind me of me when you…
- ♥ My favorite trip with you was…
- ♥ I would love to visit _____ with you
- ♥ Love is…
- ♥ Faith is…
- ♥ Strength is…
- ♥ Hope is…
- ♥ Success is…

Table 10 Sample chore list

Name (Father)	Name (Mother)	Name (Child, 7 years old)	Name (Child, 16 years old)
1.) Mow the lawn	Laundry	Pick up mail daily	Take out trash
2.)Pay the bills	Grocery shopping	Set table	Do dishes daily
3.) Clean up after dog	Carpool	Feed dog	Rake leaves off lawn

Sample chore list

Table Sample discipline chart

Misbehavior	Consequence
Stalling—not going to bed on time	Earlier bedtime
Fighting with sibling over toy	Removal of toy and time-out
Talking back	Time-out (& written amends for older child)
Breaking curfew	Earlier curfew next time
Destroying property	Work to pay for damages
Ditching school	Extra chores or school work

NOTE: Some of these forms of misbehavior are milder and others more severe, as are the corresponding consequences.

Sample discipline chart

References

Besharov, D. J. (1990). *Recognizing Child Abuse: A Guide for the Concerned.* New York: Free Press.

County of Los Angeles/Department of Health Services (2004). *The Basics about Child Abuse: A Professional's Guide.* Los Angeles, CA: The California Department of Health Services.

Miller, A. (1997). *The Drama of the Gifted Child: The Search for the True Self.* New York: Basic Books.

Muller, W. (1992). *Legacy of the Heart: The Spiritual Advantages of a Painful Childhood.* New York: Fireside.

Newman, B. M. & Newman, P. R. (1999). *Development Through Life: A Psychosocial Approach*, 7th ed. Belmont, CA: Brooks/ Cole.

Printed in the United States
45974LVS00002B/31-48